The Random Book of...

ROBERT

Max Leonard

The Random Book of…

ROBERT

Well, I didn't know that!

All statistics, facts and figures are correct as of March 31st 2009.

Published By:

Stripe Publishing Ltd
First Floor, 3 St. Georges Place, Brighton, BN1 4GA

Email: info@stripepublishing.co.uk
Web: www.stripepublishing.co.uk

First published 2009

A catalogue record for this book is available from the British Library.

10-digit ISBN: 1-907158-09-X
13-digit ISBN: 978-1-907158-09-4

Printed and bound by Gutenberg Press Ltd., Malta.

Editor: Dan Tester
Illustrations: Jonathan Pugh (www.pughcartoons.co.uk)
Typesetting: Andrew Searle
Cover: Andy Heath

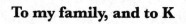

To my family, and to K

INTRODUCTION

If a landlord shouted, "Phone call for Robert!" into a crowded bar in 1950s Scotland, ten pairs of eyes might have looked up.

Replace 'publican' with 'bellboy' and a Scottish pub with a Manhattan hotel bar of the same era and you'd have witnessed a stampede. The name has been in favour for a thousand years and, although its popularity is slightly on the wane, it may well be around for another thousand.

Is having a popular name a blessing or a curse?

Roberts reading this will have a better idea than I do – although Maxs are getting more numerous. The assumption is that a Robert or a Tom (in an entirely unscientific survey the most frequent name in my mobile's contact list) gets lost in the crowd, subsumed into uniformity.

The 400 or so Roberts herein would beg to differ.

I hope this book is as fun to read as it was to write.

Max Leonard – March 2009

ROBERT

The boy's name **Robert** comes from Old German, *hrod* meaning 'fame' and *beraht* meaning 'bright'.

Rupert is an old German variant of the name. Other unusual variants and diminutives of Robert include Robin, Dobbin, Rip, Rab, Bo, Bertie and Rotberti, which was the medieval Latin variation.

Roberta was a popular female version of the name, especially in the US, but it is now rare. Other feminine forms include Robertina and Bobbie.

In Britain, Robert has been a popular name since the Middle Ages. In 1148, around one in twenty men in London was called Robert, according to the Winton Domesday Book.

One in 99 boys born in England and Wales between 1944 and 1994 was called Robert.

Born	Robert rank	Number	Most popular
1944	5th	11,315	John
1954	6th	12,398	David
1964	9th	11,112	David
1974	14th	6,759	Paul
1984	13th	6,337	Christopher
1994	25th	3,506	Thomas

In 2004 Robert appeared at number 60 on the list.

In Scotland, Robert is more popular. In 2004, 167 boys were called Robert and 166 called Robbie, placing them 43rd and 44th respectively in the top 100 names.

There are currently more than 1.7 million Roberts listed in the American phone book, which makes it the second most popular boys' name in the United States. Florida has the most Roberts, closely followed by California, Pennsylvania, New York and Texas.

In Scrabble the name Robert would score you eight points, if it were allowed.

FIRST ROBERTS

1611   **Robert Barker** prints the King James Bible for the first time, standardising worship across the country. Barker's lofty position as the King's Printer did not save him from debtors' prison, where he died. The Bible he printed is still read today.

1772   **Robert Jones**, an Englishman, publishes *A Treatise on Skating* in 1772, the first known account of figure skating. His stiff-upper-lip style is incredibly formal and inelegant and bears little resemblance to modern figure skating.

1890   **Robert Browning** is the first writer to have his voice recorded – and the first to be heard after death. The master of the dramatic monologue records part of his poem *How They Brought Good News from Ghent to Aix* on to a wax cylinder at a dinner party in 1889. The poet dies soon after, and his friends reunite in Venice the following year and listen to the recording.

1963   **Bob Charles**, a talented New Zealander, is the first left-handed player to win a PGA golf event when he takes the Houston Classic.

1965   **Bob Knox** is the first substitute in an English league football match to score a goal. The 1965/66 season was the first in which substitutes are allowed to replace injured players. Later in the same season, Knox comes off the bench once again, this time to replace his keeper, becoming the first substitute ever to save a penalty.

1978   Louise Brown, the world's first 'test-tube baby' is born in Oldham at 11.47pm on July 25th. She owes her life to **Dr. Robert Edwards**, a pioneer in reproductive medicine and in-vitro fertilisation. Since then, more than 1.5 million children have been born using IVF.

1993   With comic partner David Baddiel, **Robert Newman** is the first comic act to play – and sell out – the 12,000-seater Wembley Arena.

1998   **Robbie Earle** scores Jamaica's first-ever World Cup goal, against Croatia. English-born Earle was called up, once, to the England squad before he decided to play for Jamaica in 1997.

2001   **Robbie Hunter** becomes the first South African to compete in the Tour de France.

<hr />

NORMAN ROBERTS

Although the name **Robert** existed in Britain in an Anglo-Saxon form, it was popularised by the Norman conquests. William the Conqueror's father was called Robert, as was his son, so it must have been a shrewd political move to like the name.

The first Robert in the family, however, was **Rollo the Viking**, who came to France in the Norse invasion of 885. Rollo converted to Christianity, took the baptismal name **Robert** and ruled the coastal lands we now know as Normandy. As William the Conqueror's great-great-great grandfather, King Rollo is a direct ancestor of the current British royal family.

William the Conqueror's father was known as **Robert the Magnificent**, because of his love of opulence and fine clothes. It was not until his older brother's death that Robert became Duke of Normandy. Many suspected he had his

brother murdered, earning him the alternative nickname
Robert the Devil.

He died returning from a pilgrimage to Jerusalem, leaving
his eight-year-old illegitimate son William to succeed him.

Robert the Devil is also the subject of a medieval legend,
possibly inspired by Robert the Magnificent. As the story
goes, Robert's mother invokes the devil to help her conceive
a child. Robert, the devil's progeny, lives a life of terror
before repenting and confessing to the Pope. Depending on
whose version you believe, Robert the Devil either becomes
a pious hermit or emperor of Rome.

William the Conqueror's son had the epithet **Robert
Curthose**, meaning 'Robert Short-stockings', a term of
derision. William preferred his son William Rufus over
Curthose, choosing the younger boy as his successor
in 1087. Given that Robert had instigated a rebellion
against his father in Normandy, the decision is entirely
understandable.

SAINT ROBERTS

There are no Roberts in the Bible – given the name's German provenance, this is not altogether surprising. However, several Roberts have become saints.

Saint Robert Bellarmine was born in Montepulciano, Italy, in 1542. A fearsome member of the Roman Inquisition, he played a part in condemning Giordano Bruno to death. Bruno, an early scientist, was burned at the stake as a heretic.

Robert also lent his name to Bellarmine jugs, a type of large 'witch bottle'. Tradition has it that a witch bottle, filled with urine or toenail clippings (your own) and buried in the garden, will protect you from harmful spirits and evil spells.

Robert of Molesme, who died in 1111, was a much nicer chap. A pious man, he gathered a group of hermits together (by definition, a tough job), and founded the Cistercian Order of monks in France.

Saint Robert of Newminster founded the Cistercian abbey of that name in Northumberland. His belt, given to him by Saint Bernard, is said to have miraculous properties and resides, with his relics, in the church at Newminster. When Robert died, his friend, Saint Godric, saw his soul, surrounded by fire, lifted to heaven by angels.

St. Robert is also a small town in the Ozarks, Missouri.

ROBERT'S BODY PARTS

Robert's Arm is in Newfoundland and Labrador, Canada. It's a small town, formerly called Rabbit's Arm, whose inhabitants boast of a monster (rather unimaginatively named Cressie) in nearby Lake Crescent.

Robert's ear is, or was, in Parliament. In 1731, **Robert Jenkins** was sailing the brig *Rebecca* home from the West Indies, when it was boarded by the Spanish *guarda costa*, whose commander cut off one of his ears.

Arriving home, Robert complained about his treatment to the king, but the story doesn't really get going until 1738, when Jenkins went to the House of Commons and showed his shrivelled severed ear to MPs. The incident – which caused uproar and was perceived as an affront to the nation's honour – provoked the War of Jenkins' Ear, which lasted from 1739 until 1748.

Prime Minister **Sir Robert Walpole** was criticised for his poor showing in the war. This may have contributed to his downfall – two years in – in 1741.

Robert's Head is in Cork, Ireland. Apparently, it's a great place to fish for mackerel.

Robert's chest is in Blois, France. Jean-Eugène Robert took his Persian wife's surname and found fame as **Jean-Eugène Robert-Houdin**, the father of modern conjuring.

He used his magic chest (which now resides in the museum dedicated to his memory in Blois, his home town) to help the French emperor Napoleon III suppress a revolution in colonial Algeria.

In Algeria, wizards called *marabouts* were eating glass and performing magic tricks to exert their power over the natives and to stir up anti-French unrest.

Robert-Houdin's task was to quell rebellious feelings by proving that French magicians were superior to the locals. As a climax to his act he used the power of thought alone to make his wooden travelling chest, lifted moments earlier by a mere child, too heavy for the strongest Algerian to budge. Of course, the Algerians weren't told about the electromagnet in the bottom, which, when activated, anchored it to the floor.

Three more illusions practised by Jean-Eugène Robert-Houdin:

- Ethereal Suspension (making an assistant float)
- The Bullet Catch (catching a bullet fired from a gun in his teeth)
- The Inexhaustible Bottle (a bottle of wine that never empties)

Ehrich Weiss, a young Hungarian-American magician and escapologist, paid tribute to Robert-Houdin by taking the stage name Harry Houdini.

MAGICAL ROBERTS

Born in 1926 – the year Houdini died – **Robert Robbins** was an Australian magician who used the stage name Merlini. As a young novice, Robert hypnotised his 12-year-old sister Irene using a bicycle lamp and a *Teach Yourself Hypnosis* book. When his mother demanded he release her from the trance, he realised he didn't know how to – he hadn't reached that bit yet.

Robbins was also skilled at animal training. He had three ducks which, when not joining him on stage, lived in his garden and guarded his house.

Etienne-Gaspard Robert was known by the stage name Robertson. In the 1800s he helped to develop phantasmagoria, a sort of cinematic live-action ghost show, involving projecting images of people on to screens, or smoke, using mirrors.

Cedric Diggory, the strong, silent Hufflepuff quidditch captain and Harry's love rival for the affections of Cho Chang, is played in the fourth *Harry Potter* movie by **Robert Pattinson**.

ROBERT: THE RADIO

Roberts Radios, established in 1932, is a family business based in Yorkshire. In the early days the boss's wife used to wind the aerials by hand.

———⊰◆⊱———

RICH-LIST ROBERTS

There is quite a gap between the richest Robert and Warren Buffet, the world's richest man, who has an estimated $62 billion.

The five richest Roberts alive in 2008, as estimated by *Forbes* magazine, are:

1. **Robert Kuok**, an 84-year-old Malaysian, can claim to be the richest man in south-east Asia. He made his $9 billion in agriculture.
2. **Robert Rowling**, an American, is 153rd on Forbes's rich list. Using oil money from the family firm, he bought hotels and a gym chain, and has a $6.2 billion fortune.
3. **Robert Bass** has an estimated net worth of $5.5 billion. In 1994 he sold the Plaza Hotel, New York, to Donald Trump.
4. **Robert Holding** started his career running a Wyoming hotel and gas station. He now owns three refineries, 1,000 miles of pipes and 2,600 petrol stations and is worth $5 billion.

5. **Robert Ziff**, valued at $3.5 billion, inherited his father's publishing empire with his brothers. They now run investment companies and hedge funds.

There was also an American philosopher and artist named **Robert Ziff**. Better known as Paul Ziff, he died in 2003.

THE SUNDAY TIMES RICH LIST

Who would have thought Toblerones and cheap Benny Hedgehogs could be so profitable? Thanks to them, **Robert Miller** tops all other Roberts in the 2008 *The Sunday Times* Rich List of the richest Britons. His £850m – which places him 89th – comes from the Duty Free Shoppers chain, which he co-founded.

Hendon-born **Robert Earl** (312th/£260m) owns the Planet Hollywood restaurant chain. He is also involved in a bottled-water venture with Sylvester Stallone, and owns a stake in Everton Football Club.

Robert Plant is the highest-placed musical Robert on the list (969th/£80m).

MORE RICH ROBERTS

Ted Turner, born **Robert Edward Turner III**, founded CNN, the first 24-hour cable news station. He owns around two million acres – an area larger than the states of Delaware and Rhode Island combined – which makes him America's largest landowner. He also owns some 40,000 buffalo, the country's largest buffalo herd, some of which he sells as burgers in his chain of restaurants known as Ted's Montana Grills.

Robert Paulig owns Robert's Coffee, the Finnish version of Starbuck's or Caffè Nero. He also makes products such as coffee shampoo and coffee soap.

Robert Maxwell was born Ján Ludvík Hoch in Czechoslovakia in 1923. Fleeing the Nazis, he arrived in Britain, penniless, in 1940, and became a decorated war hero. Briefly a Labour MP, he rose to prominence in the 1980s as the owner of the Mirror newspaper group.

In 1991 he went missing from his luxury yacht off the Canary Islands and his body was eventually recovered from the sea. After his death it became clear he had 'borrowed' massively from his companies' pension funds to keep them afloat. Some 32,000 of his employees, including Anne Robinson and Alastair Campbell, lost their Mirror Group pensions. Many people, including a former *Mirror* journalist, have suspected his murder at the hands of various secret intelligence services. Victor

Ostrovsky, an ex-Mossad agent, alleged that Maxwell had also worked for the Israeli secret service and that Mossad had killed him.

In a 2007 BBC drama, Maxwell, played by *Poirot*'s David Suchet, is shown peeing from the roof of the *Mirror*'s buildings onto the street below.

Robert L. Johnson is the first African-American billionaire. He founded the Black Entertainment Television (BET) network, which launched in 1980 and initially broadcast for only two hours a week.

In 1968, American chainsaw millionaire **Robert McCulloch** won London Bridge. The City of London had put it up for auction as it was sinking into the Thames and was structurally unsound. He took it apart stone by stone and shipped it to Arizona, where it was reconstructed as a tourist attraction.

Robert's bid of $2,460,000 represented twice the estimated dismantling costs ($1.2m) plus one thousand dollars for each year of his life at the time he hoped to have the rebuilding finished.

The bridge is recognised as the world's largest antique by the *Guinness Book of Records* – it was classified as such to avoid being taxed.

Robert Simpson is president of Jelly Belly. Each year, his company sells more than 16 billion jelly beans in hundreds of flavours, and makes more than $107m. Simpson – whose first job was a gravedigger in a pet cemetery at the age of 15 – has said that his favourite flavours are pink grapefruit and toasted marshmallow.

Why a wanted fugitive would steal a chicken sandwich and a sticking-plaster when he had $500 in his pocket is incomprehensible. Yet this is exactly what cross-dressing billionaire **Robert Durst** did in Pennsylvania in 2001. The policeman attending the shoplifting discovered that Durst had earlier been arrested shortly after a black bag containing his chopped-up 71-year-old neighbour was found floating in Galveston Bay, Texas. Durst, whose father was a property mogul, absconded before trial. Claiming self-defence, he was acquitted of murder in 2003.

⟐

ROBERT: THE CRATER

Robert is a small crater on the slopes of Mons Vitruvius, the ninth-tallest mountain on the moon. It's just between the Sea of Tranquility and the Sea of Serenity, so do pop by if you're ever in the area.

ASTRONAUT ROBERTS

Roberta Lynn Bondar was Canada's first female astronaut, and the first neurologist in space. She spent eight days, one hour and 44 minutes in space in 1992.

The top-five astronauts called Robert, ranked by how long they have spent in space:

NAME	NATIONALITY	SPACE TIME
Robert Curbeam	American	37d 14h 33m
Robert Lee 'Hoot' Gibson	American	36d 0h 15m
Robert L. Crippen	American	23d 13h 46m
Roberto Vittori	Italian	19d 18h 47m
Robert A. Parker	American	19d 6h 52m

SOME ROBERT-RELATED BRITISH PLACES

NAME	DESCRIPTION	LOCATION
Robert Irvine's Skerries	Rocks	Shetland Islands
Robert's Crooie	????	Orkney
Robert Law	Hill	South Lanarkshire
Robert Ness	Promontory	Argyll and Bute
Robert's Seat	Hill	North Yorkshire
Roberttown	Town	West Yorkshire
Robert Hall	Stately home	Lancashire
Robert Tait's Hill	Hill	Shetland Islands
Robert's Farm	Farm	Buckinghamshire
Robertland	Ruined castle and estate	East Ayrshire

Robertsbridge	Town	East Sussex
Roberton Mains	Village	South Lanarkshire
Robertsend	Village	Worcestershire

ROBERTS IN LYRICS, PART I

If you're down he'll pick you up, Doctor Robert.
Take a drink from his special cup, Doctor Robert.
Doctor Robert, he's a man you must believe,
Helping everyone in need,
No one can succeed like Doctor Robert.

Doctor Robert, the Beatles song on the album Revolver,
has numerous drug references in it. Some people say
the title refers to Dr. Robert Freymann, who was known
for prescribing generous amounts of amphetamines to
celebrities and who lost his licence to practise medicine
in 1968. It has also been speculated that Bob Dylan is
the mysterious doctor, since he introduced the band to
marijuana. John Lennon once joked that he himself was
Doctor Robert, as he carried the band's pills on early tours.

MORE DOCTOR ROBERTS

The most famous photo of the Loch Ness Monster was taken by **Dr. Robert Kenneth Wilson**. Showing a dinosaur-like head and neck emerging from ripples on the loch's surface, the so-called 'Surgeon's Photo' has been hotly disputed ever since. Wilson himself maintained its veracity to his grave.

Recently declassified documents reveal that **Dr. Bob Ballard**, the marine explorer who found the wreck of the RMS *Titanic*, was actually on a secret US Navy reconnaissance mission. He asked the Navy to fund a search for the lost cruise ship, but was told that he'd have to locate two nuclear submarines, the USS *Thresher* and USS *Scorpion*, first.

Both subs disappeared in mysterious circumstances in the 1960s. Although there are persistent rumours that the *Scorpion* was scuttled by a Soviet attack, it was, according to Bob, probably hit by one of its own torpedoes. The *Thresher*, meanwhile, probably imploded when a pipe burst in its engine room.

When the covert mission was finished, Bob had only 12 days left to find the *Titanic*, but examining the submarine wrecks had given him a good idea of what the *Titanic*'s trail of debris might look like. On September 1st 1985, Bob's robotic submersible, the *Argo*, discovered the *Titanic*'s final resting place, about 400 miles off Newfoundland.

Dr. Robert Hyatt has spent a good portion of his life designing chess computers. His first, called Blitz, played its opening move in 1968; Cray Blitz, its successor, won the World Computer Chess Championship twice, something that the most recent, Crafty, has yet to emulate.

Dr. Robert Woo, a dental surgeon in Washington, found himself in a lot of trouble in 2006 when a practical joke backfired. He temporarily implanted fake boar tusks into a patient's mouth while she was under anaesthetic. The patient – who was also his assistant – eventually saw the photographs, quit her job and sued Dr. Woo.

Woo's insurance company refused to cover him for the prank, so Woo settled with his assistant for $250,000... and then sued the insurance company! The case went all the way to the US Supreme Court who ruled, in a 5-4 decision, that the practical joker be compensated $750,000, plus the $250,000 settlement he had originally paid out.

Dr. Robert Jarvik helped to invent the Jarvik 7, the world's first completely artificial heart designed to sustain human life long-term. The first heart, which required the patient to be wired to equipment the size of a shopping trolley, kept its recipient alive for 112 days. The longest anybody has survived with a Jarvik 7 is 620 days.

Dr. Robert, known to his family as Bruce Robert Howard, is the lead singer of the Blow Monkeys. The group became famous in the 1980s and found time to record with Jamaican singer Eek-a-mouse and soul legend Curtis Mayfield.

When, in 2003, **Dr. Robert Atkins** slipped on an icy step outside his New York apartment and hit his head, it was a great loss to weight-conscious celebrities everywhere. The diet guru's controversial regime of steaks, bacon, cheese and other fatty, carb-free foods have helped millions including Geri Halliwell, Victoria Beckham and Al Gore lose weight – so much so that Stevie Nicks of Fleetwood Mac called him "a god among men".

Later, a leaked medical report showed that the doctor, the son of a restaurateur, weighed 18 stone, meaning that, having followed the Atkins diet for 39 years, he was clinically obese when he died. His supporters claimed that the extra weight was due to fluid retention while in hospital and that the report was leaked to blacken his reputation.

ROBERTS ON THE TITANIC

Here are five of the many Roberts listed on the official
register of the deceased from the RMS *Titanic*, which sank
on April 14th 1912, killing 1,517 people:

NAME	CLASS	OCCUPATION	AGE	LAST ABODE
Robert Guest	3	Labourer	23	London
Robert Reeves	Crew	Fireman/Stoker	30	Southampton
Robert Knight	2	Fitter	39	Belfast
Robert Allan	Crew	Bedroom Steward	36	Hampshire
Robert W. N. Leyson	2	Engineer	25	London

Robert W. Daniel climbed aboard lifeboat three. He is
the only passenger called Robert recorded as being picked
up by the RMS *Carpathia*, which saved 705 lives that night.
He was joined in that lifeboat by **Robert Couper** and
Robert Triggs, stokers on the ship.

ROBERT: THE BIKE, PART I

Bob Jackson opened his first bike workshop in 1935 using money borrowed from his mum. Today, the Bob Jackson marque still makes bicycles by hand in Yorkshire, although its founder died in 1999.

⟫◆⟪

COPS AND ROBERTS

Policemen are known as 'Bobbies' and 'Peelers' after **Sir Robert Peel**, the Conservative politician who, while home secretary, helped to create the first modern police force in the Metropolitan Police Act of 1829. The first policemen wore blue tailcoats and top hats.

Sir Robert Anderson, an Irishman, was an assistant commissioner at Scotland Yard during the Jack the Ripper investigations. Anderson variously maintained that the culprit of the Whitechapel murders had already been apprehended and was in a mental asylum and that it was "a definitely ascertained fact" that the murderer was a Polish Jew. Nobody before or since has been so sure.

NEWGATE ROBERTS

The Newgate Calendar was originally a monthly record made
by the Keeper of Newgate Prison in London. Subtitled *The
Malefactors' Bloody Register*, it detailed inmates' gory crimes
as they passed through the prison gates for the last time
– on their way to Tyburn gallows. A five-volume edition,
which included tales of notorious criminals such as Dick
Turpin, became a literary hit towards the end of the 18th
century. Children were encouraged to read it for their moral
edification – or at least so they'd be too scared to stray off
the straight and narrow.

Top 10 Roberts in *The Newgate Calendar:*

1. **Robert Emmet**. "Executed for High Treason,
    20th of September 1803." Emmet, the 'Darling of
    Erin', was an Irish Nationalist who led an abortive
    uprising in Dublin. He was captured when he
    broke cover to see his sweetheart, Sarah Curran.
    The Crown, fearing weaknesses in its case, bought
    off Emmet's lawyer, Leonard Macnally. In return
    for £200 and a pension, the crooked lawyer gave
    the prosecution access to all his papers.

2. **Robert Harpham.** "Under the Pretence of
    making Buttons he made Coins, and was executed
    at Tyburn, 24th of May, 1725."

3. **Robert Kingshell**. A "daring plunderer" and
    one of the so-called "Waltham Blacks": "Having
    blackened their faces, they went in the daytime

to the parks of the nobility and gentry, whence they repeatedly stole deer, and at length murdered the Bishop of Winchester's keeper on Waltham Chase." Kingshell was executed at Tyburn in December, 1723.

4. **Robert Powell**. "A Starving Fortune-Teller, who was convicted by the Middlesex Magistrates of being a Rogue and Vagabond, 1807."

5. **Robert Aslett**, assistant cashier of the Bank of England. "Condemned to Death for embezzling Exchequer Bills to a Large Amount." He was reprieved at his Majesty's Pleasure in November 1804.

6. Daniel and **Robert Perreau**. "Twin Brothers, who, though popularly believed to be innocent, were executed at Tyburn, 17th of January, 1776, for Forgery."

7. **Reverend Robert Foulkes**. "Executed 31st of January, 1679, for the Murder of his newly-born Babe."

8. **Robert Creighton, Baron of Sanquire**. "Executed in 1612 for the Murder of John Turner, who had accidentally put out one of his Eyes." After the Baron lost his eye in a fencing accident, he plotted Turner's death for five years. Eventually, he found a willing assassin – named **Robert Carliel** – who shot Turner while drinking in a pub.

9. **Robert Ladbroke Troyt**. "A Boy of Seventeen, executed before Newgate, 28th of November, 1798, for Forgery, his First Offence."

10. **Robert Alsop**. A midshipman, he was convicted alongside six seamen, "for committing a Riot in the City of London, and impressing a Citizen thereof." They were, however, but treated leniently "in order that they might fight against France."

MOBERTS

Gangsters called Robert...

Robert Trimbole was known as 'the Godfather' in his native Australia. He died in Spain in 1987 while on the run from a conspiracy to murder charge.

Roberto Pannunzi (b. 1948) is part of the Calabrian mafia, the 'Ndrangheta, a name deriving from Greek that means 'honoured society'. Pannunzi was arrested by Spanish police with his son in 2004. A fugitive since 1999, he was believed to be the 'Ndrangheta's biggest drug trafficker, smuggling up to two tons of cocaine into Europe every month.

'Uncle' Bart is the vicious loan shark played by **Bob Hoskins** in the film *Unleashed* (aka *Danny the Dog*). Hoskins also plays a gangster in the classic British film *The Long Good Friday* and was one of Brian de Palma's first choices to play Al Capone in *The Untouchables*, a part which eventually went to **Robert De Niro**.

Robert De Niro (b. 1943) made his name in gangster movies, mainly playing New York mafia mobsters. He appears in two of the American Film Institute's Top Ten gangster movies of all time. The AFI defines the 'gangster' genre as focusing on organised crime of maverick criminals in a 20th-century setting. De Niro's gangster filmography:

Bloody Mama (1970)
Mean Streets (1972)
The Godfather, Part II (1974)
The Untouchables (1987)
Goodfellas (1990)
Casino (1995)
Heat (1995)
Analyze This (1999)
Analyze That (2002)
Shark Tale (providing the voice of Don Lino – 2004)

Robert Shaw played Doyle Lonegan, the Irish crime boss stung by **Robert Redford** and Paul Newman in *The Sting* (1973).

Robert F. Carrozza, aka **Bobby Russo**, is a Boston mobster who, in the 1990s, was accused of masterminding an internecine war from his prison cell while jailed on racketeering and corruption charges.

American actor **Robert Loggia** has the gravelly voice of a mobster. He has lent it to characters in the *Grand Theft Auto* and *Scarface: the World is Yours* video games, and also to Sykes, Dickens's brutal moneylender, in Disney's animated *Oliver & Company* (1988). He has played numerous mobsters, most notably in *The Sopranos* and in David Lynch's *Lost Highway* (1997).

Robert Carey is associated with characters such as Fred 'Killer' Burke and Raymond 'Crane Neck' Nugent, and was a member of the Egan's Rats gang, which terrorised the city of St Louis in Prohibition-era America. Although never named by police, he was a suspect in the St Valentine's Day Massacre of 1929, a shootout between Al Capone and Bugs Moran that took the lives of seven men.

Rocco Cammeniti, the not-so-friendly Erinsborough mobster in *Neighbours*, is played by Italian-Australian actor **Robert Forza**.

"Cops Gun Down **Robert Salve**" proclaimed the headlines in Indian papers in August 2008. Robert, alias Rahul Raju, wheeled and dealed in the city of

Pune, fighting his way up the crime ranks and becoming notorious in 2003 for shooting at a cop. He was killed, while reportedly on his way to murder a Madam, as part of the Police Commissioner's 'bullets for gangsters' initiative.

Roberto Saviano is an Italian journalist who wrote *Gomorrah*, a book exposing the dealings of the *Camorra*, the Neapolitan mafia. A 2008 film, which used non-professional actors and locals to dramatise the book, resulted in a Camorran gangster being arrested. Giovanni Venosa, who played a gangster called 'Giovanni', was ratted on by disgruntled underworld associates after they spotted him during a screening in an Italian jail.

Saviano, only 27 when the book came out, has received death threats because of his stand against organised crime.

<hr/>

KILLING ROBERTS

Roberto Succo was an Italian serial killer who claimed his first victims, his mother and father, at the tender age of 19, after they refused to lend him the family car. Succo served five years in a psychiatric hospital then escaped in May 1986. He killed and kidnapped his way across France, Italy and Switzerland until he was caught again in his home town of Mestre, on the Venetian mainland. In March 1988, during an escape attempt, Succo fell from the prison roof. He survived, only to commit suicide two months later.

Succo killed at least three police officers during his crime spree. French police picketed a stage play based on his life, and objected to the film, *Roberto Succo* (2001), on the grounds that they glorified the cop-killer.

Robert Englund is better known as Freddie Krueger, the knife-fingered slasher in the *Nightmare on Elm Street* films. Englund also auditioned for the part of Luke Skywalker in *Star Wars*. When he didn't get it, he encouraged his friend Mark Hamill to go for the role.

Robert Chambers, a former altar boy, was known by the press as 'the preppie killer' because of his clean-cut looks and the private schools he'd attended on scholarship. He strangled a girl he met in a bar and then claimed she had tied him up with her panties and forced him to have sex with her, and that she'd died accidentally as he freed himself. Chambers was 6ft 5ins, over a foot taller and almost twice as heavy as his victim.

In 1678, Sir Edmund Berry Godfrey, an English magistrate, was found strangled and impaled on his own sword on what is now Primrose Hill in London. On unreliable evidence, and probably motivated by anti-Catholic sentiment, **Robert Green**, Henry Berry and Lawrence Hill were charged with the crime.

Coincidentally, Primrose Hill – where the murder took place and where Green, Berry and Hill were eventually hanged – was known at the time as Greenberry Hill.

Michelle Kosilek was called **Robert Kosilek** when she was convicted of killing her wife, Cheryl, in 1990. She changed her name in 1993 and, though anatomically a man, lives as a woman in an all-male prison. She is suing the US Department of Correction to force them to pay for a sex-change operation, claiming that not to do so constitutes cruel and unusual punishment.

Robert William Pickton is a Canadian pig farmer and serial killer. He killed six women and is charged with the murder of a further 20, many of whom were prostitutes he hired to perform at the *Piggy Palace Good Times Society*, a non-profit organisation he ran. It is thought he fed many of the victims to his pigs.

In 1995, **Robert Brecheen**, a murderer, was on death row in Oklahoma, awaiting execution. He was due to be put to death in the middle of an August night, but at 9pm the guards coming to lead him away could not wake him. Brecheen had somehow taken an overdose of sedatives in a suicide bid. Undeterred, officers revived him and pumped his stomach before leading him off for lethal injection. The state-directed killing took place two hours late.

Roberts In Lyrics, Part II

A fictional **Robert Moore** appears on Nick Cave and the Bad Seeds' critically acclaimed album, Murder Ballads, from 1996.

Well, Robert Moore stepped up and said:
"That woman is my wife."
And he drew a silver pistol,
And a wicked bowie knife;
And he shot the man with the wing-nut ears
Straight between the eyes
And Betty Coltrane, she moaned under the table.

In addition to the man with the wing-nut ears, Robert also kills a sailor with mermaid tattoos and a frog-eyed man – all of whom claim to be married to the bigamous Betty.

Hanging Roberts

The post of hangman was a very desirable job, right up until hanging was abolished in 1964.

Robert Ricketts Evans 1873-1875
Robert never actually officially hanged anyone, but used to invite people to his house and, when drunk, perform a mock hanging upon them, in full costume. He is also rumoured to have imprisoned his daughter in a cell in his courtyard, only for her to elope with her Hungarian lover.

Robert Wilson 1920-1936
A Mancunian, Wilson assisted at 47 executions.

Robert Orridge Baxter 1915-1935
Baxter assisted at 53 executions and was principal hangman
at 44.

Robert Leslie Stewart 1950-1964
Assisted at 20 executions between 1952 and 1958, when
he was made a principal. He went on to execute five more
people, and was on the Home Office's final official list.

━━◆◆◆◄━━

PIONEERING ROBERTS

An intensely brilliant man, **J. Robert Oppenheimer**
put his intellect to deadly use: he was scientific director
of the Manhattan Project, the top-secret US programme
that developed the atomic bomb. Observing the first test
detonation, Oppenheimer claimed to be reminded of some
lines from the sacred Hindu text the *Bhagavad Gita*: "If the
radiance of a thousand suns were to burst at once into the
sky, that would be like the splendour of the mighty one…
Now I am become Death, the destroyer of worlds."

In 1831 **Robert FitzRoy**, the captain of a small surveying
ship called HMS *Beagle*, was preparing for a long journey
into southern waters. He requested that a gentleman
naturalist be posted on board so he might have some decent
dinner conversation to alleviate the boredom of the voyage.

A young Charles Darwin took the position and the voyage became the basis for *The Origin of the Species*, in which he proposed the theory of evolution. The two men fell out bitterly after its publication.

FitzRoy continued to work for the Admiralty and developed groundbreaking theories of meteorology to warn ships of coming storms. He became the world's first proper weatherman, and coined the phrase 'weather forecast'. In 2002, the British Isles sea area, Finisterre (made famous by the BBC Radio 4's shipping forecast), was renamed FitzRoy in his honour.

Dr. Robert Homer Simpson is another pioneering meteorologist. He co-developed the Saffir-Simpson Hurricane Scale, which rates hurricanes on a scale of one to five. A category five hurricane has winds in excess of 156mph (250kph) and a storm surge bigger than 18ft (5.5m).

American **Robert J. Flaherty** made the world's first commercially successful documentary film, *Nanook of the North*, in 1922. The film followed an Inuit and his family in the Canadian Arctic. For the filming he asked Nanook (real name: Allakariallak) to re-enact some scenes from Inuit life – getting him to hunt with spears instead of his usual gun – sparking a debate about the nature of documentary 'reality' which has yet to be resolved.

Flaherty knew the Inuits from the previous year when he'd visited them to make a different film. His first effort was unfortunately destroyed when he accidentally dropped a cigarette end on to the highly flammable film negative and it caught fire.

Robert Boyle was one of the foremost natural philosophers of the 17th century. He formulated Boyle's Law, which states that for a fixed amount of gas at a fixed temperature, volume and pressure are in inverse proportion.

Although he is regarded as one of the first modern chemists, he came from the alchemic tradition, and believed in the possibility of turning base metals into gold.

Robert Hooke was a 17th-century polymath who worked with Boyle on his gas experiments, and also has his own law – Hooke's law of elasticity. Less well known is his work as an architect. He surveyed the City of London with Christopher Wren after the Great Fire of 1665, and designed the Bethlem Royal Hospital, the notorious madhouse better known as Bedlam.

Hooke's *Micrografia*, a treatise on microscopy, was a groundbreaking biological work. Likening a plant's structure to a monk's cell, he was the first to use the word to describe the basic unit of life.

In 1839, Alexander Grant and **Robert McVitie** cooked up the recipe for one of the nation's favourite biscuits – the digestive. It was so named because it contains bicarbonate of soda, an antacid, which soothes the stomach. Digestives are also made with wholemeal flour, which helps to keep you regular.

It was McVitie's son, also called **Robert McVitie**, who made the bakery a household name. He studied baking in Paris and Vienna and won a gold medal and first-class certificate for his craft in the Calcutta exhibition of 1883-4.

The chocolate digestive was first baked in 1925; McVitie's did not introduce the Hob Nob until 1985.

Pirate Roberts

Famous pirates called Robert, in chronological order:

Robert Searle
Terrorised: ...Jamaica, c.1660,
Infamous for: ...general swashbuckling and buccaneering.

Robert Culliford
Terrorised: ... the Nicobar Islands and Île Sainte-Marie, c. 1696.
Infamous for: ... being William Kidd's first mate, and mutinying against the famous pirate.

Bartholomew Roberts

Terrorised: ... the Caribbean, Brazil, Newfoundland and
Africa, 1719-1722.
Infamous for: ... capturing an estimated 470 ships. 'Black
Bart' was perhaps the most successful pirate ever.

Robert Surcouf

Terrorised: ... France and afar, 1792-1801.
Infamous for: ... fighting the British as a corsair and
capturing 47 ships.

Roberto 'El Pirata' Cofresi

Terrorised: ... Puerto Rico, 1818-1825.
Infamous for: ... being generous and sharing his spoils
with the poor. Cofresi sold his soul to the devil, in order to
"defeat men and be loved by women".

Robert Newton

Terrorised: ... Hollywood, 1950.
Infamous for: ... playing Long John Silver in Disney's
Treasure Island. His performance and accent set the template
for all pirates since.

The Dread Pirate Roberts

Terrorised: ... Guilder and Florin, 1973 and 1987.
Infamous for: ... never leaving his captives alive. He kidnaps
Princess Buttercup in William Morgenstern's book, *The
Princess Bride*, and Rob Reiner's film of the same name.

It transpires that Roberts is Buttercup's long-lost love, the farm boy Westley, and the name 'Dread Pirate Roberts' is simply a franchise passed from man to man designed to inspire terror in all who hear it.

Robert Maynard, on the other hand, is a famous pirate killer. A lieutenant in the Royal Navy, he ambushed the infamous Blackbeard and engaged him in battle. Maynard and Blackbeard duelled, the pirate taking 20 cutlass wounds and five pistol shots before he fell. Maynard then beheaded him, tied the head to his bow and sailed with it back to New Hampshire, where it was hoisted on a pole at the mouth of the Hampton River, as a warning to other pirates.

Slang Roberts

Bob

1. A colloquial name for a British pound sterling, and, in some parts of the United States, for a dollar coin. Originally, however, it meant a British shilling. The name is possibly derived from 'bawbee', which was 16th-century slang for a halfpenny.
2. Rhyming slang for marijuana in some parts of the world. **Bob Hope** = dope.
3. Can also refer to marijuana, or a large conical spliff, in reference to **Bob Marley**.
4. Is an acronym for 'battery-operated boyfriend', referring to a sex toy or vibrator.

5. Stands for 'Born on Board', naval slang for a crewman born on a military ship.

6. Is the Dutch equivalent of Des, the designated driver who won't drink of an evening out. It comes from a Dutch drinking-awareness campaign phrase, *Bewust Onbeschonken Bestuurder*, meaning 'conscious, non-drunk driver'.

7. Stands for Bombs Over Baghdad, the title of an anti-war single released by hip-hop group Outkast in the year 2000.

'Bob's your Uncle' is a common phrase expressing the simplicity with which something can be accomplished. It is said to date back to 1887, when the British Prime Minister, **Robert Gascoyne-Cecil, 3rd Marquess of Salisbury**, appointed his nephew Arthur James Balfour as Minister for Ireland. Balfour then referred to the PM as "Uncle Bob" in conversation, causing an outcry in the press.

Although he went on to be prime minister himself, Balfour was rather inexperienced at the time, hence the suggestion that things happen more easily if Robert is your mother's brother. The flaw in this theory is that the first recorded use of the phrase is in 1937.

Much beloved of teak-coloured antique-loving TV Yorkshiremen, the phrase "It's a **Bobby Dazzler**" denotes something that is striking or exciting in appearance. It is particularly prevalent in the north of England.

Bobby Dazzler is also the name of an Australian sitcom starring singer John Farnham as **Bobby Farrell**, an up-and-coming musician. It ran for 14 episodes in 1977-8.

≡➤◆◆◆◆◆◆◆≡

Heroic Roberts

Several Roberts – English and Scottish – contributed to the 'Heroic' era of Antarctic exploration.

Robert Falcon Scott led a team of explorers including Ernest Shackleton on the first official British National Antarctic expedition between 1901 and 1904. A Scotsman, William S. Bruce, was rejected from the British expedition so he set up a privately financed Scottish one that sailed in 1902.

The Scottish expedition included:

- Botanist **Robert Neal Rudmose Brown**
- **Robert Mossman**, in charge of meteorological and magnetic studies
- **Thomas Robertson**, who captained the *Scotia*, the expedition's ship
- **Robert McVitie**, of McVitie's biscuits, who donated £50 to the expedition

Scott is better known for his second Antarctic expedition which was beaten to the South Pole by Roald Amundsen, a Norwegian. Scott's team perished of cold and starvation only 11 miles from their food stores while returning from the Pole. Scott's final diary entry read:

"For my own sake I do not regret this journey, which has shown that Englishmen can endure hardships, help one another, and meet death with as great a fortitude as ever in the past."

An expedition in 1956 found a tin of Edam cheese left by Scott in the snow 44 years earlier. When it was opened the cheese was still fit to eat.

When it comes to the North Pole, Roberts have had better luck – or have they? **Robert Edwin Peary**, an assistant and four Inuit men were the first people ever to make it to the North Pole, on April 6th 1909. Nobody on the expedition except Peary knew how to navigate, and, since Robert took no proper navigational measurements and also edited his diaries extensively for publication, his achievement has been much in doubt ever since.

On a separate expedition, in 1900, Peary lost eight toes to the cold.

"Take a step forward, lads, it'll be easier that way." Thus spoke **Robert Erskine Childers** as he faced the firing squad in 1922. Childers, an Irish nationalist, was executed by the Irish Free State while appealing against a conviction for carrying a firearm without a licence. He shook hands with every single gunman before accepting the inevitable.

More Famous Last Words From Roberts

"All fled, all done, / So lift me on the pyre: / The feast is over, / The lamps expire."
Robert E. Howard, writer and creator of *Conan the Barbarian*, in a suicide note left in his typewriter, upon hearing of his mother's death in 1936.

"Strike the tent."
Robert E. Lee, Confederate General in the American Civil War.

"Do I look strange?"
Robert Louis Stevenson, author.

"You can be a king or a street sweeper, but everybody dances with the grim reaper."
Robert Alton Harris, a career criminal who killed two boys in 1978. His words, recorded by Warden Daniel Vasquez shortly before he was gassed in 1991, were a reference to *Bill and Ted's Bogus Journey*, released the previous year.

"I am the head of the *Luftwaffe*, but I have no *Luftwaffe*."
Robert Ritter Von Greim, fallen *Luftwaffe* chief, upon taking a cyanide pill in 1945.

"Money can't buy life."
Bob Marley.

ROBERT: THE BIKE, PART II

Roberts Bicycles have been hand-built in Croydon for more than 50 years.

<hr/>

RAILWAY ROBERTS

Robert Davidson designed and built a miniature electric locomotive, the world's first, in 1837. In 1842, a full-size version called the Galvani sped along at four miles per hour, although it was not powerful enough to carry passengers or freight. Its zinc batteries made it 40 times more expensive than a coal-powered steam locomotive, a fact which did not stop a group of steam engineers from taking out the competition by smashing the Galvani in its shed.

Another railway pioneer, **Robert Stephenson,** is less well known than his father, George, whose portrait now adorns the £5 note. Robert was a partner in the Newcastle workshop that built the Locomotion, the steam engine that made the inaugural journey by steam from Shildon to Stockton in 1825. He also helped to survey the line, but was working in South American goldmines when the Locomotion made its historic journey on the world's first railway.

On June 8th 1968, a special three-carriage train set out from New York, bound for Arlington Cemetery, Washington, carrying the body of **Robert F. Kennedy**.

Robert's assassination was blamed on Sirhan Sirhan, a mentally unstable Palestinian but, as with his brother's death, conspiracy theorists maintain there were sinister forces at work. In the frame: Dave Morales, an enormous Native American who hated Robert because he believed the Kennedies hung the CIA out to dry during the failed Bay of Pigs invasion of Cuba in 1961. Nevertheless, official investigations still maintains Sirhan's guilt and finds no evidence of a second gunman.

The train took seven hours to reach its destination, as a million ordinary Americans lined the tracks to pay their respects to the dead Kennedy.

———◆———

INVENTING ROBERTS

A Scotsman, **Robert William Thompson**, was the original inventor of the pneumatic tyre. He patented the idea for 'Aerial Wheels' in France in 1846 and the USA in 1847, the same year he demonstrated the idea in Regent's Park. He also invented highly useful items such as the ribbon saw, the portable steam crane, the elliptical rotary engine… and the self-filling fountain pen.

So why don't all our cars roll on Thompsons? Robert became frustrated that there wasn't rubber thin enough for his purposes and turned his attentions to solid rubber tyres. It was only after the bicycle was invented that John Boyd Dunlop popularised the pneumatic tyre. Dunlop was granted a patent in 1888 but two years later was informed that it was invalid.

At the local branch of Kwik Fit, in Robert's birthplace, Stonehaven, there is a memorial in tribute to the Scottish genius.

Robert Kearns also did his bit for the development of the motorcar. He patented his design for intermittent windscreen wipers in 1967. Despite taking his invention, which allowed car drivers to set how frequently the wipers wiped, to various American car manufacturers, none licensed it from him. Soon, though, Ford, Chrysler and others began offering wipers which paused between swipes, and Kearns sued.

Kearns eventually received $10.2m from Ford, and $18.7m from Chrysler. Much of the money went on legal fees, and Kearns said he only fought so hard to defend the integrity of the patent system.

On February 26th 1935, **Robert Watson-Watt** demonstrated radar technology for the first time. Radar superseded the vast concrete listening posts that still dot the British coastline as the first means of detecting incoming aircraft, giving the country time to prepare itself for attack. The technology would prove vital in the Second World War.

As World War II progressed, scientists found a way of jamming radar signals using a device called a magnetron. Many years later, **Robert Hall** invented an improved version of the magnetron that made microwave cookery possible. Hall also invented the semi-conductor injection laser, now used in compact disc and DVD players, laser printers and supermarket barcode readers.

In 1954 **Robert Adler** made the couch potato's life a lot easier. The Space Command, which he co-invented, was the world's first proper TV remote control.

Dr. Robert Moog invented the Moog analogue synthesizer, the first widely used electronic musical instrument.

Moog's synthesizers were used by jazz pioneer Herbie Hancock and by the godfathers of electronic music, Kraftwerk, as well as more mainstream acts such as David Bowie and ABBA. One of the best-known uses of the Moog (which is pronounced like 'vogue') is in the closing solo on Lucky Man, from Emerson Lake and Palmer's eponymous debut album in 1970.

Some other famous records featuring Moogs:

- Pisces, Aquarius, Capricorn & Jones, Ltd. (1967) – The Monkees
- Abbey Road (1969) – The Beatles
- Talking Book (1973) and Innervisions (1974) – Stevie Wonder
- I Feel Love (1977) – Donna Summer
- Moon Safari (1998) – Air

A Moog was also used to create the eerie soundtrack to Stanley Kubrick's 1971 movie *A Clockwork Orange.*

Robert F. Borkenstein of the Indiana State Police invented the Breathalyzer in 1954, ending half a century of unreliable drunkenness tests including walking along the white line while reciting the alphabet. Simply falling asleep in the police station was sometimes considered proof of overindulgence. The Breathalyzer was smaller and more easy to use than his first crack of the whip, the 'Drunkometer', which was the first machine that could reliably detect and measure blood alcohol. Borkenstein also did some early development work on the lie detector.

Robert H. Cobb, a Hollywood restaurateur, put his name on the menu with a tasty salad he invented when struck by the midnight munchies in the 1930s. Very much of the 'everything goes' school of cookery, the Cobb salad combines lettuce, tomatoes, turkey, bacon, hard-boiled eggs, avocado, chives, Roquefort cheese and special vinaigrette. Some versions of the Cobb salad can contain up to 1,500 calories a serving; the recipe has been criticised by nutritionists for being highly calorific and fattening.

So much of modern life would be unthinkable without **Robert Noyce**. Known as the 'Mayor of Silicon Valley', Noyce co-invented the integrated circuit, a forerunner of the microchip, in 1959.

ROBERTS IN LYRICS, PART III

Bobby Mugabe, boss of Zimbabwe,
Where do you go from here?
Bobby Mugabe, someone is softly
Whispering in your ear.

By 1988 it was clear even to a German electro-pop band
called Froon that **Robert Mugabe**, Zimbabwe's first
democratically elected leader, was overstaying his welcome.
Blaming ex-colonial powers bent on regime change for the
country's woes, Mugabe has since presided over a corrupt
regime and has tortured and killed political opponents, their
families and their supporters. Meanwhile, due to disastrous
agricultural policies, crops have failed and the economy has
nosedived. In June 2008, official figures put Zimbabwean
inflation at 11,250,000%.

OTHER RULING ROBERTS

King Robert of Naples, also called **Robert the Wise**,
was celebrated as a patron of the arts. Thanks to his
beneficent reign, from 1309 until 1343, he was known as
'the peacemaker of Italy'.

My kinda town! The first mayor of Barrie in Ontario,
Canada was called **Robert Simpson**. He was also a
master brewer and he established a fine lakeside brewery in
Barrie that still bears his name.

Carlos Roberto Flores first served in the Honduran government in the 1980s under President **Roberto Suazo Cordóva**, before taking the top job himself in 1998. During his presidency, the Central American republic was hit by Hurricane Mitch, which devastated much of the country.

Carlos Roberto Flores' predecessor in the post was called **Carlos Roberto Reina**.

The first President of the USA to be called Robert will also be the last. In the comic strip *Judge Dredd*, **President Robert L. Booth** rigs an election to get the job in 2068 and then precipitates the Atomic Wars, which devastate America and allow the Judges to come to power. When captured, he is sentenced to 100 years in suspended animation in Fort Knox, but in 2029, he escapes…

Robert Kocharyan was elected the second President of the Republic of Armenia after its independence from the Soviet Union in 1998. Kocharyan was born in the town of Stepanakert, which lies in present-day Azerbaijan.

Jaime Gerardo Roberto Marcelino María Ortiz Lizardi was known to the people of Argentina as **Roberto María Ortiz**. He was president from 1938 until 1942, during Argentina's so-called 'Infamous Decade'.

ROBERTS IN LYRICS, PART IV

Bobby Shafto's gone to sea,
Silver buckles on his knee;
He'll come back and marry me,
Bonny Bobby Shafto!

Bobby Shafto's bright and fair,
Combing down his yellow hair;
He's my love for evermore,
Bonny Bobby Shafto!

Bobby Shafto, immortalised in the folk song and nursery rhyme, is probably **Robert Shafto**, an 18th-century MP from County Durham. He was a handsome gadabout who used the name 'Bonny Bobby Shafto' while electioneering.

The song recounts the story of how Robert broke the heart of one Bridget Belasyse when he married another woman, Anne Duncombe. Bridget is said to have died two weeks after hearing the news. As Bobby is reputed to have spent all Anne's personal fortune, Bridget may have had a lucky escape.

Political Roberts

Democratic Senator **Robert Carlyle Byrd** has served in the US Senate since January 3rd 1959, making him the longest-serving and oldest member of that house.

In 1978, while Majority Leader of the Senate, Byrd recorded and released an LP of old-time country music called *US Senator Robert Byrd: Mountain Fiddler*. Until he developed a medical condition known as an essential tremor, Byrd would sometimes entertain the Senate with his fiddle during breaks.

Robert McNamara helped to introduce the seatbelt, when working on injury-prevention research for Ford.

His later injury-prevention work, however, was mixed. He was the US Secretary of Defence who helped avert nuclear war during the Cuban Missile Crisis in 1962. Some American generals were gung-ho, and Fidel Castro had already given the order to launch the nuclear warheads if attacked, but McNamara and the Soviet leader Nikita Krushchev delicately negotiated peace behind closed doors. On the debit side, McNamara was one of the principal architects of US involvement in the Vietnam War – which saw 58,193 Americans, and hundreds of thousands of Vietnamese, killed.

PRIME MINISTER ROBERTS

Sir Robert Walpole (1676-1745) is generally recognised as Britain's first prime minister although, in his day, the term 'prime minister' was one of abuse. In office between 1721 and 1741, Walpole was given 10 Downing Street as a gift from King George II, where he moved in 1735. Walpole is distantly related to Horatio Nelson.

Robert Jenkinson, second Earl of Liverpool (1770-1828), is the longest-serving British PM after Sir Robert Walpole. He took the job between 1812 and 1827.

Sir Robert Peel (1788-1850), he who founded the police force, went on to become prime minister twice: for four months between December 1834 and April 1835, then from August 1841 until June 1846.

Robert Arthur Talbot Gascoyne-Cecil, Third Marquess of Salisbury (1830-1903), was prime minister three times, serving for a total of 13 years. His final stint in the job saw him become the first PM of the 20th century.

Robert Menzies (1894-1978) was Australian prime minister for two terms. He won his second term in 1949, and is the longest occupant of the post.

Robert Hawke (b. 1929) was the 28th prime minister of Australia, between 1983 and 1991. Hawke won four consecutive elections but his legislative achievements were, for many Australians, overshadowed by his prowess in the pub. He downed a yard of ale (2.5 pints) in 11 seconds. The feat, which was included in the *Guinness Book of Records*, took place in the Turf Tavern, Oxford, while Robert was a Rhodes Scholar in 1963.

Robert Borden (1854-1937) was the Conservative prime minister of Canada who led the nation through the First World War.

Robert Muldoon (1921-1992) was New Zealand's elected leader from 1975 until 1984; before that, he was an accountant.

Robert Themptander (1844-1897) was Sweden's fourth prime minister, between 1884 and 1888, during the reign of King Oskar II.

Robert Fico (b. 1964) has been prime minister of Slovakia since July 2006. He is very anti-media and has labelled some of the newspapers in his country 'prostitutes'. Despite, (or maybe because of) this, he has been voted Slovakia's most trusted politician.

Sir Robert Bond (1857-1927) was prime minister of
Newfoundland between 1900 and 1909. Newfoundland did not
become part of Canada until 1949, the last province to do so.

JAMES BOND ROBERTS

When Ian Fleming died in 1964, his publishers were
reluctant to let the popular James Bond series of books die
with him. They invented **Robert Markham**, a pen name
for other writers to use when writing Bond novels. The only
Robert Markham Bond novel ever published was called
Colonel Sun, written by Kingsley Amis in 1968.

Robert Davi is an American character actor, best known
for his turn as a gangster either in the 1989 Bond flick
License to Kill, or as Jake Fratelli (the singing gangster) in
1980s kids classic *The Goonies*. He's also played those on the
other side of the law, most notably in the TV series *LA Law*,
or as an FBI Agent in *Die Hard*.

Robbie Coltrane, born **Anthony Robert McMillan**,
rebelled against his conservative upbringing and was almost
expelled from prestigious boarding school Glenalmond
College for hanging prefects' gowns from the clock tower.
Robbie's stage name pays homage to John Coltrane; the
portly jazz lover's first Bond appearance was as Russian
mafia boss Valentin Zukovsky in *GoldenEye* (1995), a role he
reprised in *The World is Not Enough* (1999).

Robert Carlyle joined **Robbie Coltrane** in *The World is Not Enough*, the 19th Bond film. They first appeared together, however, in ITV's *Cracker*, in which Carlyle played a distraught Hillsborough victim. Carlyle left school without qualifications and worked as a decorator with his dad until he bought Arthur Miller's play *The Crucible* with some book tokens and decided acting was for him.

Robert Braithwaite was 597th in the *Sunday Times* Rich List 2008 and has an estimated £130m fortune. He owns Sunseeker, the company whose yachts have featured in three Bond movies including *Casino Royale*.

The second-ever person to play James Bond was **Bob Holness**. He took the part in a South African radio adaptation of *Moonraker* in 1956, at the age of 28.

(The first person to play 'Jimmy' Bond was Barry Nelson in *Casino Royale* in 1954.)

When not impersonating a secret agent, Bob has been a radio presenter and host of the game shows *Take a Letter* (in 1961), *Call My Bluff*, *Raise the Roof* and, most famously, *Blockbusters*.

Blockbusters ran on ITV from 1983 until 1993, principally to give bored students something to do in the afternoons. In the early half of its run, the line "I'll have a 'P' please Bob" would cause widespread hilarity whenever it was used. This was superseded after the second summer of love by the more knowing "I'll have an 'E' please Bob".

It was once claimed that Bob Holness played the saxophone on Gerry Rafferty's version of Baker Street. Although false, the factoid became an urban myth, and something that Bob has played up to on numerous occasions.

<hr/>

MORE QUIZMASTER ROBERTS

In his long TV and radio career, **Robert Robinson** presented *Call My Bluff*, *Ask the Family* and *Brain of Britain*. It was also on his watch that the word 'fuck' was first said on British TV – in 1965 by Kenneth Tynan on late-night chat show *BBC-3*.

Bob Barker was the American Leslie Crowther. He presented the US version of *The Price is Right* for 35 years, recording his final episode in 2007 at the age of 83.

Robert Kilroy-Silk is best remembered for his long-running eponymous chat show, which started with a public debate on nudity in 1986 and ended in ignominy, cancelled in 2004 after its host wrote an article calling Arabs "suicide bombers, limb amputators and women repressors". He then went on to present *Shafted*, a quiz show that was widely ridiculed and was dropped from the schedules after just three episodes in 2001.

Four years after his death in 2003, a ghostly **Bob Monkhouse** reappeared on British TV screens. The presenter of *Celebrity Squares*, *Family Fortunes* and *Bob's Full House* was reanimated in an advert raising awareness of prostate cancer. "What killed me kills one man per hour in Britain," he quipped. "That's even more than my wife's cooking." Bob was well loved for his one-liners. Previously he had joked: "I want to die like my father, peacefully in his sleep, not screaming and terrified, like his passengers."

Bob's break in radio came when he got his RAF superior, a psychiatrist, to sign without reading a letter to the BBC stating that Corporal Monkhouse should be given an audition to boost his confidence.

In 1995 he was distraught when two of his joke books, containing a lifetime's material, went missing. Bob put up a £10,000 reward and the books were returned 18 months later.

MORE FUNNY ROBERTS

Robert Newman followed the time-honoured route to
comedy stardom, from Cambridge to BBC Radio to BBC
2, in *The Mary Whitehouse Experience* with Hugh Punt, Steve
Dennis and David Baddiel. Newman and Baddiel then
created the blockbusting *...in Pieces* sketch show. Although
Rob didn't totally shun his comedy fame, he stepped out of
the limelight to write several novels, and now campaigns on
environmental issues.

Also progressing from Cambridge to the BBC, **Robert
Webb** was a member of the Footlights amateur dramatic
club. While starring as Prince Charming in *Cinderella*, the
Christmas panto, he met David Mitchell (who was playing
Tom the Page Boy). They went on to make a little-seen sketch
show on cable TV and *That Mitchell and Webb Sound* on BBC
Radio 4 before crossing into primetime TV with *Peep Show*.

Rob once claimed he wanted The Macarena played at his
funeral.

When technical problems hit *The All New Alexei Sayle Show*,
comedian **Bobby Chariot** would hold things together
until normal service could be resumed. Chariot, who
looked suspiciously like Sayle, had the catchphrase "How
ya diddling" and a propensity to lapse into melancholia –
telling sob stories about his ex-wife and his drink problem.
Unsurprisingly, his less-than-funny slots usually ended with
Chariot cursing the audience: "Bloody sod ya then!"

Rob Brydon, who's made a career playing hapless characters in unsettling comedies such as *Marion and Geoff*, had a brief stint as a presenter on the Home Shopping Network before the comedy career took off.

Rob is also the resident Tom Jones expert on the BBC Radio Four panel show *I'm Sorry, I Haven't a Clue*.

Robert Nankeville, who got his big break on *Live From Her Majesty's* in 1983, is more widely recognised as **Bobby Davro**. His father, Bill Nankeville, was a champion distance runner, holding the mile record, running with Roger Bannister and competing in the 1948 and 1952 Olympics. Nevertheless, Bobby's sporting genes did not help him on Channel 4's *The Games*, which pitted celebrities against each other in Olympic-style contests. He failed to achieve a medal placing in the 2003 show.

Brummie funnyman **Robert Norman Davis**, better known as Jasper Carrott, is the father of Lucy Davis, better known as Dawn from *The Office*. In 2006, thanks to Jasper's OBE, Lucy was allowed to get married in St Paul's Cathedral.

More AKA Roberts

REAL NAME	ALSO KNOWN AS	PROFESSION
Robert Beck	Iceberg Slim	Writer
Spangler Arlington Brugh	**Robert Taylor**	Actor
Robert LeRoy Parker	Butch Cassidy	Wild West outlaw
Edgar Gaines	**Bobby Blake**	Retired gay porn star, now an ordained Christian minister
Robert Bruce Banner	The Incredible Hulk	Scientist/rampaging giant
Timothy McVeigh	**Robert Kling**	Oklahoma bomber
Robert James Ritchie	Kid Rock	Rock star

Deborah Sampson Gannet isn't the most likely sounding Robert, but she took the name on in order to enlist to fight the British in the American War of Independence. As **Robert Shurtliff**, she joined up to the 4th Massachusetts Regiment, where the other soldiers assumed she was a boy too young to grow a beard.

Robert/Deborah received a bullet-cut to the head and two musket balls in the thigh, which she treated herself using a penknife so that her secret would not be discovered. She remained on active duty until she came down with a fever and a doctor discovered the band she used to bind her breasts. He told George Washington, who summoned Robert and honourably discharged her without ever publicly disclosing her sex.

Motorcycle stuntman **Robert Craig 'Evel' Knievel** was a daredevil from an early age. After dropping out of school, he was fired from his job as a construction worker when he wheelie-d an earthmover into a pylon, leaving his home town without power for several hours.

An incurable romantic, Knievel married his childhood sweetheart, Linda Bork, who only agreed after he kidnapped her three times.

Some stunts by Evel Knievel:

YEAR	VENUE	JUMP	OUTCOME
1967	Las Vegas	141ft over the fountain at Caesar's Palace Hotel	Crashed, leaving him in a 29-day coma
1973	Los Angeles	50 stacked cars	Success
1974	Snake River, Arizona	The Snake River canyon on a steam-powered Sky Cycle	Failure. Knievel came up short but parachuted safely to the bottom of the canyon
1975	Wembley Stadium	13 single-decker buses	90,000 people watched him crash, breaking his pelvis

Evel's son, **Robbie Knievel**, surpassed his father in 1999 when he jumped the Grand Canyon, a feat that Evel had never been allowed to attempt.

ROBIN – ROBERT? – HOOD

There is no conclusive proof that Robin Hood ever existed outside medieval ballads, literature, TV and film. If he did, however, several Roberts are candidates to have been the real Hood.

The earliest evidence Robin might have actually existed is from Yorkshire pipe rolls, a type of financial record, mentioning a **Robert Hood**, fugitive, nine times between 1226 and 1234.

In nearby Wakefield, at around the same time, lived a **Robert Hood** and his wife Matilda, who is commonly thought to be the inspiration for Maid Marion.

There is also a certain **Robert FitzOoth** of Locksley, Nottinghamshire. However, an 18th-century Hood fanatic, desperately looking for proof of Robin Hood's existence in old papers, may have made FitzOoth up.

Finally, in Kirklees Priory there stands a memorial stone bearing the inscription (in Medieval English):

Here underneath this little stone,
*Lies **Robert, Earl of Huntington**.*
Never was there archer as he so good,
And people called him Robin Hood.
Such outlaws as he and his men,
Will England never see again.
Died 24th December 1347.

However, the stone dates only from the 18th century, although it is supposedly a copy of an older piece. And, like much of the other evidence, it would make Robin Hood a Yorkshireman.

Two royal documents from 1417 refer to **Robert Stafford**, a Sussex chaplain, who assumed the alias of Frere Tuk.

❯❯◆❮❮

REBELLIOUS ROBERTS

In 2006, four years after dying in mysterious circumstances, **Robert Guéï**, coup leader and former president of the Ivory Coast, was finally laid to rest in the capital, Abidjan. Guéï, a general, had seized power in a military coup in 1999, but was shot in the head in another attempted coup in 2002. The Ivorian government claimed that Guéï was killed while leading the uprising, whereas the United Nations suspected that he had been summarily shot.

In 1861 **Robert Smalls**, a mixed-race slave working on a Confederate military ship in Charleston, South Carolina, found himself alone in charge when the ship's white officers went ashore for the night. He took the opportunity to hoist the white flag and sail himself, his family and the other slaves on board to freedom – directly to the Union vessels blockading the port. He became a national hero and later sat in the US House of Representatives.

Rob Roy MacGregor, sometimes known as Scotland's Robin Hood, became an outlaw in the Scottish Highlands after, being deceived out of some money, he was forced to default on a loan given to him by one of the local Lairds. Earlier in his life, Rob had joined the Jacobite uprising against the English, guaranteeing his place in Scottish folklore.

Daniel Defoe wrote a book on Roy, which made him a legend in his own lifetime and he was played in a 1995 film by Liam Neeson.

To make a Rob Roy cocktail, a variant on the Manhattan, add Scotch whisky to Vermouth and bitters then stir through some ice.

⬛◆⬛

GUNPOWDER, TREASON AND PLOT

One of the biggest failed plots in history was carried out by a gaggle of Catholic Roberts.

Robert Catesby masterminded the scheme to blow up the anti-Catholic King James I, on the opening day of Parliament; November 5th 1605. His intention was to install the nine-year-old Princess Elizabeth on the throne as a Catholic head of state.

Catesby was assisted by **Robert Wintour** and **Robert Keyes**, but an anonymous letter warning prominent Catholics away from Westminster did for them all. The letter was shown by another Robert, **Robert Cecil, First Earl of Salisbury**, to King James. As punishment, the plotters were half-hanged then disembowelled while still alive.

―――≫◦≪―――

ROBERT: THE RULES, PART I

Robert's Rules of Order is a book developed by **Henry Martyn Robert** in the 1870s, after he was asked to preside over a church meeting and was embarrassed not to know how. Loosely modelling its procedures on the US House of Representatives, *Robert's Rules…* is widely used in the US and Canada for meetings of all kinds in which group decisions must be taken.

―――≫◦≪―――

SPYING ROBERTS

According to KGB files, **Robert Talbott Miller**, codename 'Mirage', was part of the Golos ring that spied for the Soviets in 1941. He had access to information inside the US Office of Naval Intelligence and the Office of Strategic Services (OSS), which would later become the CIA.

A secret joint operation between the FBI and Scotland Yard codenamed 'Lighthouse' put **Robert Hendy-Freegard** behind bars in 2005. Robert pretended to be a secret agent and conned a dozen people out of around £1m over a ten-year period.

The conman convinced his victims he worked for MI5 and that he required their money in the national interest. He gained access to their bank accounts and asked them to prove their loyalty to him through a series of bizarre tasks: he made one woman hide in a bathroom for a week.

Another victim was told to sleep on park benches and in airport terminals, and forced to subsist on £1 a week. Robert also seduced several of his female victims and subjected one man, who believed he was to infiltrate an IRA cell, to a beating in order to "toughen him up".

Meanwhile, Robert was spending their savings on expensive cars, suits and five-star holidays in Brazil. Detective Superintendent **Bob Brandon** of the Metropolitan Police described him as "the most accomplished liar I have ever encountered in 25 years in the police".

The former car salesman, 34, was convicted of two counts of kidnap, ten charges of theft and eight counts of deception at Blackfriars Crown Court in London. He is now spending the rest of his life detained at Her Majesty's pleasure.

FBI agent **Robert Hanssen** spied on the US for the Soviet Union and Russia for an estimated 22 years. He received more than $1.4m in cash and diamonds for his information, in what the US Department of Justice called "possibly the worst intelligence disaster in US history."

Despite a trail of rash moves and compromised situations, the FBI did not catch up with Hanssen until they paid a Russian informer $7m for Hanssen's KGB file. They finally swooped on their man as he left a bin-bag full of classified material under a bridge in a Virginia park. Hanssen's lawyer negotiated a plea bargain so that his client would avoid the death penalty; nevertheless, he is serving a life sentence in solitary confinement, with no chance of parole.

Hanssen was played by Chris Cooper in *Breach* (2007), a movie based on his story.

Napoleon Solo, who fought the mysterious criminal organisation THRUSH in the kitsch 1960s TV series *The Man from U.N.C.L.E.*, was played by debonair actor **Robert Vaughn**. Vaughn also starred in *The Magnificent Seven*, alongside Steve McQueen, and more recently appeared in the BBC's *Hustle*.

Vaughn may be inadvertently responsible for the demise of *The A-Team* in 1986. He played General Hunt Stockwell, who hires the A-Team during the show's final run. It is said that die-hard fans boycotted the show because they could not accept the team would be hired by the US military, who they had been evading since 1972.

SOME FAMOUS MIDDLE-NAMED ROBERTS

David Robert Beckham – Footballer
David Robert Jones aka David Bowie – Singer
Steve Robert Irwin – Aussie naturalist
William Robert Thornton – Actor
Sir Douglas Robert Steuart Bader – Fighter-pilot ace
Jeremy Charles Robert Clarkson – Motoring know-it-all

Marion Robert Morrison was more commonly known as John Wayne. He was given the middle name Robert at birth, but his parents then changed it to Michael after they decided to name their next son Robert. Marion had a couple of movie credits in the 1920s as Duke Morrison, but became John Wayne in 1930 when starring in *The Big Trail*. Wayne wasn't even present at the discussion during which studio boss Winfield Sheehan and director Raoul Walsh decided the new name.

ROBERT: THE RULES, PART II

Bob Ciaffone is a master poker player and an expert on gambling law. He wrote *Robert's Rules of Poker* for the Poker Players' Association. Free to download, they have been widely adopted in both professional and amateur competitions.

FIGHTING ROBERTS

"Chess is better than sex," **Bobby Fischer** once said,
and it was on the chessboard that he played his part in
America's Cold War against the USSR. Considered by
many the greatest chess player who ever lived, Bobby broke
the Soviet stranglehold on the World Chess Champion title
by beating Boris Spassky in Reykjavik in 1972.

Twenty years later, Bobby spat on a US prohibition order
before a rematch in embargoed Yugoslavia, the US issued
an arrest warrant and Fischer never went home again. He
was granted Icelandic citizenship and spent his final years as
a paranoid recluse, only breaking his silence to make anti-
Semitic and, post-9/11, anti-American statements.

Bobby died on January 17, 2008, aged 54.

Panamanian **Roberto Durán**, now retired, is thought
to be one of the best boxers of all time. He held world
titles at lightweight, welterweight, junior middleweight
and middleweight, getting heavier as he got older. He was
also the second man to fight professionally in five different
decades, retiring in 2002, aged 50, with a record of 117
fights, 103 wins and 70 knockouts.

Bobby Chacon (b. 1951) was a brutal boxer who was
twice WBC world champion at featherweight. Although
initially supportive, his wife became increasingly distressed
by his profession and repeatedly asked him to quit and

move to Hawaii. When she was unable to convince him she killed herself with a rifle, the night before he fought Salvador Ugalde. Bobby won, and dedicated his triumph to his wife's memory.

When **Robert Meier** died in 2007, Germany lost its oldest man and one of its last surviving soldiers of the First World War. In 2006, the 109-year-old met with Henry Allingham, at 110 Britain's oldest surviving veteran. Maurice Floquet, 111, France's oldest veteran, was too frail to travel but sent his regards.

Bob Braham, real name John Randall Daniel Braham, was the most decorated RAF airman of the Second World War. He claimed at least 29 enemy aircraft destroyed, and six more damaged.

Air ace and test pilot **Robert Stanford Tuck** distinguished himself flying Spitfires and Hurricanes in the Battle of France and the Battle of Britain. Shot down over Boulogne, he was a POW for two years, but survived the war.

Tuck's exemplary career was marred by one extraordinary piece of bad luck. Shooting at a German bomber headed for Cardiff, he forced the enemy to jettison its cargo early. One bomb caught the corner of an army training camp, detonating and killing one man – Tuck's sister's husband.

Robert E. Lee came from a war-faring family: his father was a Major General nicknamed 'Light Horse Harry', and he was a descendant of Thomas More and **King Robert II of Scotland**. Lee took up arms against the Union in the American Civil War and was named one of the Confederate army's first five generals. He is thought by historians to be responsible for many of the heavy losses that crippled the Confederate forces at the Battle of Gettysburg in 1863.

'Fighting' Bob La Follette was a Republican Senator for Wisconsin in the United States. He was voted joint first in the 'Ten greatest senators in the nation's history' by American historians. Despite his name, he was a vocal opponent of the First World War.

⟹◆⟸

ROBERT: THE AXIS OF EVIL

During the Second World War, the name Roberto was used as a codeword by fascist sympathisers to identify each other. By saying '**RoBerTo**' as a greeting, you were communicating to the other person your allegiance to the axis of **RO**me, **BER**lin and **TO**kyo.

In 1942, 18 Italian-Americans using this greeting were excluded from the San Francisco military area because they were a security threat. The ousted fascistophiles included a publisher, a dried-fruit dealer and a former San Francisco Police Commissioner, Sylvester J. Adriano, who was also Chairman of the North Beach Draft Board.

Nazi Roberts

Professor Doctor Ernst-Robert Grawitz was a
member of the SS and the top doctor in the Third Reich.
As such, he was chief advisor to Heinrich Himmler on the
use of gas chambers and conducted terrible experiments on
Nazi concentration camp prisoners.

As the Reich crumbled, he holed up with Hitler in his Berlin
bunker. After Hitler denied his request to leave, Grawitz
killed himself and his family by detonating two grenades
under the dinner table as they ate supper.

Robert Ley was a prominent Nazi politician, head of the
German Labour Front (DAF) from 1933-45. Ley was a
notorious womaniser who freely embezzled from the DAF
to fund villas, cars and a valuable personal art collection.
His second wife shot herself in 1942 after a drunken brawl.

The DAF, under Ley, was responsible for the *Volkswagen*, or
the 'people's car', project, working with Ferdinand Porsche to
design what the world would later know as the VW Beetle.

Ley hung himself while awaiting trial in Nuremburg in
October 1945.

Robert 'Bazi' Weiß was a daredevil fighter pilot who
flew Focke Wulfs, mostly over the Western Front against the
Allies. He notched up 121 victories and downed 12 Spitfires
before being shot down by the Norwegians in 1944.

Robert-Richard Zapp was a deadly Nazi U-boat commander. He sank 106,000 tons of Allied shipping and was awarded the Knight's Cross in 1942. He was so successful that he eventually commanded his own 'Zapp' naval regiment.

<hr/>

ROBERT: THE SHOP, PART I

Robert Dyas is a chain of home and garden stores across the south of England.

<hr/>

LESSER-KNOWN ROBERTS

Bob Marley is a comedian from Maine in the US, who claims his father knew nothing about the reggae legend when naming him.

Robbie Williams has played in defence for Accrington Stanley since 1999. He has never faced his more successful namesake, **Robbie Williams**, a left-sided defender or midfielder who plays for League One side Huddersfield Town.

Robert Fowler won silver in the vélodrome as part of South Africa's 4000m pursuit team at the Helsinki Olympic Games in 1952, predating by 40 years a Liverpudlian Fowler's sporting achievements.

Robert L. Stevenson was the first head coach of DePaul University's basketball team. He coached the Chicagoans to eight wins and six defeats in the 1923/24 season.

―――≫◈≪―――

ANIMAL ROBERTS

The **bobcat**, Latin name *Lynx rufus*, is a large member of the cat family and the most common wildcat in North America. It has a short, bobbed tail and likes rabbits and hares, though at a pinch it will eat rodents, deer and young farm animals.

Bob Crosby was an American jazz bandleader, his most famous group being **Crosby and the Bobcats**.

Robert's Arboreal Rice Rat is, as its name suggests, a rodent that lives in trees and eats rice. Its young are called pups, pinkies, kittens or nestlings.

When John Gray, a night-watchman in Edinburgh, died of tuberculosis, his Skye Terrier was beside himself. Popular account has it that the dog, known as **Greyfriars Bobby**, stood guard unwaveringly at his grave for 14 years, until his own death in 1872. More realistically, the dog hung around near the grave and went to a local pub for meals and to keep warm.

Bobby became something of a celebrity, and a statue of him now stands in front of the Greyfriars Bobby pub. Because Greyfriar's Kirkyard was consecrated ground, Bobby couldn't be buried next to his master. He was laid to rest nearby, just inside the cemetery walls.

Bird Dog Bobby is a blues musician from Missouri who formed his band, the Honey Hounds, in 1992.

ANIMAL-STUDYING ROBERTS

Robert E. Gregg was one of the world's foremost myrmecologists. As such, he devoted his life to studying ants.

Ever wanted to know about herpetology? **Bob Irwin** is a leading herpetologist, he can tell you all about amphibians and reptiles. Studying frogs in particular is revealing about changes in the environment, and herpers, as they are known, are helping doctors to develop medicines from snake venom.

Bob is also the father of the late **Steve Robert Irwin**, the croc-loving naturalist and environmental campaigner who died in 2006.

George Robert Crotch, a coleopterist, or beetle-studier, was a world expert on ladybirds. A contemporary of Darwin, he presented the evolutionist with several samples.

CLAN BRUCE OF SCOTLAND

Robert de Brus, was first Lord of Annandale, was a
12th-century Norman marauder and founder of the Bruce
dynasty. His father (also **Robert de Brus**) came over with
William the Conqueror in 1066, and his son was...

Robert de Brus, second Lord of Annandale. Known as
'The Cadet', his eldest son was called...

Robert de Brus. Unfortunately this Robert de Brus died
before his dad, so the title went to his younger brother,
William. William's son, however, was...

Robert de Brus, who was born in 1195 and became fourth
Lord of Annandale. With Isobel of Huntingdon he sired...

Robert de Brus, fifth Lord of Annandale. Following a
succession crisis in Scotland, he was beaten to the crown by
his rival John Baliol. He had a son named...

Robert de Brus, sixth Lord of Annandale. Legend has
it that when it fell to Robert to tell a friend's widow of his
death during the Crusades, the said widow, Marjorie of
Carrick, took him prisoner and refused to let him go until
he married her. Nevertheless, they seemed happy and had a
son called...

Robert the Bruce, **King Robert I of Scotland**. Robert
the Bruce was a fearsome warrior, who became one of
Scotland's greatest kings when he killed his rival John Comyn
in 1306, before leading Scotland to independence from

England. His statue guards Edinburgh Castle and his image has adorned Scottish banknotes. Romantic novelist Barbara Cartland was a direct descendant of the Scottish king.

King Robert had a bastard son called **Robert Bruce** before dying in 1329 of an 'unclean ailment' – possibly leprosy or syphilis. The king's heart was taken on a Crusade to the Holy Land, but only made it as far as Granada. It now resides at Melrose Abbey, whereas his body is in Dunfermline.

King Robert II of Scotland, born in 1316, was Robert the Bruce's grandson.

Robert II's son was called John, and for years he was considered illegitimate because his parents were too closely related. However, when he did accede to the throne he changed his name, to become **King Robert III**. His younger brother, **Robert Stewart**, must have been nonplussed by the decision.

ROBERT: THE SHOP, PART II

Robert Fergusson is a chain selling plumbing and electrical supplies in Tasmania, Australia.

<hr />

AMERICAN PLACES CALLED ROBERT

Louisiana is the only US state that has a town called **Robert**. Here you'll find the Jellystone campsite, a Yogi Bear-themed resort.

Many other towns incorporate Robert in the name. They include: **Robertsville**, Ohio; **Waynesville-St Robert**, Missouri; and **Robertsdale**, Pennsylvania.

Robert Lee, Texas, is named after the American Civil War general.

Rob Roy, located in Fountain County, Indiana, is a small town named after the Scottish folk hero.

Robert Indiana, on the other hand, is a famous artist connected to the Pop Art movement. Indiana is usually to be found in Maine, and is best known for his huge sculptures of numbers and short words such as EAT, LOVE and HUG. He starred in Andy Warhol's film *Eat* from 1964, which is a single, 45-minute shot of Robert eating a mushroom.

MORE ARTY ROBERTS

At the heart of Swinging London in the 1960s was gallery owner **Robert Fraser**. Known as **Groovy Bob**, he was art director of the Sgt. Pepper's Lonely Hearts Club Band sleeve, suggesting to The Beatles that Peter Blake be hired to design it. The montage includes 57 life-sized cardboard photographs of celebrities, nine waxwork models loaned from Madame Tussauds, a stone bust, four statuettes and a doll wearing a jumper with "Welcome the Rolling Stones, Good Guys" written across it.

Fraser was also friends with The Rolling Stones, and his arrest alongside Mick Jagger and Keith Richards was immortalised by Richard Hamilton's famous *Swingeing London* works. Unlike the rock stars, Fraser pleaded guilty to heroin possession and received six months' hard labour. He tragically never beat his heroin addiction and was one of the first British celebrities to die of AIDS, in 1986.

Robert Rauschenberg, born Milton Ernst Rauschenberg in 1925, thought he might become a pharmacist until he discovered his artistic talent while a US Marine. He is best known for using non-traditional materials in an artistic setting. One of his most famous 'combines' from 1959 brings together a stuffed angora goat, a tyre, a police barrier, the heel from a shoe, a tennis ball and paint.

Robert Taylor is the UK's foremost aviation artist, specialising in pictures of Second World War RAF planes in action.

Bob and Roberta Smith is a contemporary British artist who lives in London. The single individual, real name Patrick Brill, reportedly chose the pseudonym after experimenting with sending diverse work to galleries under different names and personas; Bob and Roberta Smith was the first to gain notice.

Robert Capa is best known for his photographs of the Spanish Civil War. His most iconic image, *The Falling Soldier* from 1936, depicts a republican fighter falling after being shot in the chest. For years, the photo's authenticity has been doubted: was it in fact a staged photo-op, a fake?

Capa's biographer, Richard Whelan, has come up with an answer. Capa was with the troops during an informal ceasefire, so they orchestrated a battle charge for the benefit of the camera. The enemy, fearing a real offensive, opened fire and the trigger was pulled at the moment the camera shutter snapped. The man died: a real casualty of a make-believe attack.

Robert Harling worked for the famous Linotype typographic house designing fonts. His creations include Playbill, Chisel and Tea Chest.

Robert Mapplethorpe is the American photographer who shot the cover of Patti Smith's classic album, Horses. Many of his images were confrontational and homoerotic. In 1998, the vice-chancellor of the University of Central England was interviewed under caution after an art student took some photos of Mapplethorpe's work to illustrate her essay and the developers handed the negatives to the police. Concentrating on a black-and-white image of one man peeing into another's mouth, the police tried unsuccessfully to prosecute the university under the Obscene Publications Act – the same act unsuccessfully used to ban *Lady Chatterley's Lover*.

ROBERT: THE MOVIE

Bob Roberts is actor Tim Robbins's directorial debut. The satirical film from 1992 takes place during the Gulf War and tells the story of a fictional politician who, in his bid for the US Senate, uses music to portray his conservative, Christian values as rebellious. Robbins, who took the lead role as Bob and wrote the film, based the character on a sketch he'd written for *Saturday Night Live* in 1986.

MORE DOUBLE ROBERTS

Actor **Robert Robertson** found popularity as the pipe-smoking pathologist Doctor Stephen Andrews in *Taggart*. He played Dr. Andrews in 52 episodes of the detective series, having joined in the pilot episode in 1983. He was the last remaining member of the original cast when, in 2001, he died suddenly of a heart attack. He was on stage in Perth at the time, reciting the **Robert Burns** poem *Holy Willie's Prayer*.

Another **Robert Robertson** was a probable victim of the Cleveland Torso Murderer, also known as the Mad Butcher of Kingsbury. The Mad Butcher's official murder toll is 12 or 13, between 1935 and 1938, although there are a possible 40 more victims in the Ohio and Pittsburgh area killed between the 1920s and 1950, the year that Robert was found *sans* head. This makes the Mad Butcher one of the most prolific serial killers in history. His (or her) identity, however, was never established.

Robbie Roberts is a gay porn star who has a picture of Thumper from Bambi tattooed on his chest.

In 2007, **Robert Robertson** crashed his plane just metres from oncoming traffic on a Florida freeway. He'd been flying a cargo of shoes and clothing to Nassau in the Bahamas when the engine cut out shortly after take-off.

Despite cartwheeling out of the sky and the whole front of the plane being destroyed, Robertson survived with only a couple of broken bones and a cut to the head. He was found by fire crews, dazed and disoriented, still sitting in the pilot's seat.

Kathryn Robert Robertson was born in Scotland in 1899 but spent her life in Hollywood. She used the name Kay Riehl, although she appeared mostly uncredited, in films such as *Sabrina* (starring Humphrey Bogart and Audrey Hepburn) and *A Star is Born* (with Judy Garland and James Mason). She finished her career in popular 1960s TV shows such as *Dragnet* and *The Fugitive.*

Robbie Robertson was one of the founding members of, and the chief songwriter in, The Band. They rose to prominence after backing **Bob Dylan** on his legendary 1965-66 tour, his worldwide 'coming out' as an electrified musician – during which an audience member in Manchester called Dylan 'Judas'.

The Band then went on to release the classic albums Music from Big Pink (named after the pink house they'd rented near Woodstock) and The Band. They retired from touring on Thanksgiving Day in 1976, after a concert filmed by Martin Scorsese as *The Last Waltz*, and split up soon after.

Robertson did not join his former band members when they re-formed in 1983. He did, however, continue his association with Martin Scorsese, working on the soundtracks to movies from *Raging Bull* to *The Color of Money* to *Casino*.

Robert Roberts was butler to influential American politicians in the 19th century. He wrote *The House Servant's Directory: A Monitor for Private Families* which became, in 1827, the first book by an African-American to be commercially published in the United States.

Bob Roberts played for the West Bromwich Strollers FC in the 1870s in various outfield positions, despite an observer commenting: "As a forward he was useless, and as a half-back, or back, he could stop a man but invariably missed the ball."

It was only after the club changed its name to West Bromwich Albion in 1880 that he found his vocation keeping goal. 'The Prince of Goalkeepers', or 'Long Bob', as he was known, helped the Baggies to an FA Cup victory in 1888 over Preston North End and in 1887 became the club's first international player, winning a total of three caps for England.

Joseph 'Robbie' Robertson is a high-ranking staffer at the *Daily Bugle*, second in command and close confidant to J. Jonah Jameson, the editor who employs Peter Parker and has an antagonistic relationship with Spider-Man.

Robertson, one of the first serious African-American characters in comic books, first appears in *Amazing Spider-Man* #51 in August 1967. He is often the voice of reason in Jameson's campaign to discredit Spider-Man.

He also appears in the animated TV series and is played by Bill Nunn in all three of Sam Raimi's films starring Tobey Maguire.

———

CARTOON ROBERTS

Despite looking like the sort of sponge you might use to scour dishes, Nickelodeon's **SpongeBob SquarePants** was actually designed and drawn by a marine biologist, Steven Hillenburg.

Created by David McKee, the animator who also drew Mr. Benn, ***King Rollo*** starred the eponymous child-king, his cat, Hamlet, the Magician, Cook and Queen Gwen. Like *Mr. Benn*, *King Rollo* only ran for 13 episodes. During his short reign, Rollo did regal things such as learn to tie his shoelaces, take a bath and tidy the royal bedchamber, while much of the actual ruling was done by Cook and Hamlet.

Robert Crumb, underground comics maestro and the creator of Fritz the Cat, Keep on Truckin' and Devil Girl, worked on greetings cards and kids' trading cards before his breakthrough success, *Zap*. It almost never saw the light of day as the original artwork was stolen by its first publisher. Luckily, Crumb had photocopied it before he sent it off.

Bob Monkhouse was a talented artist who was a paid contributor to *The Beano* and *The Dandy* from the age of 15. Young Bob didn't have to work for a living, however: his prosperous family ran a custard factory.

Bob Kane created the DC Comics superhero Batman. His inspirations included Errol Flynn's portrayal of Zorro, Leonardo Da Vinci's ornithopter flying machine and a film from 1930 called *The Bat Whispers*. Bob's original plan, influenced by the success of Superman, was to have red flashes on Batman's costume. It fell to Bill Finger, a writer, to suggest Batman's black and grey colours, as well as other refinements. Batman first appeared in *Detective Comics #27* in 1939.

Bob the Builder first appeared on British TV screens in 1999. Since then, Bob, voiced by Neil Morrissey, has had two number-one hits: Can We Fix It? swiped the Christmas number-one spot in 2000 and Bob's cover of Mambo No. 5 followed up in 2001.

After many builders and parents voiced concerns about Bob's adherence to safe working practices, later programmes saw Bob don protective eye-glasses when doing dangerous jobs.

Robert Frederick 'Bob' Godfrey was a British animator with an instantly recognisable ink-and-marker-pen style. He was responsible for drawing the classic children's series *Roobarb & Custard* and *Henry's Cat*.

Godfrey also made risqué adult animations, including *Henry 9 to 5*, which won a Bafta in 1971. The short features a bowler-hatted commuter who escapes from the drudgery of daily life into sexual daydreams. Although never seen in the kids' cartoons, there seems little doubt the laconic yellow moggie is his.

⟫◆⟪

ROBERT: THE BULLET

The .257 Roberts is a medium-powered rifle cartridge designed in the 1920s by Ned Roberts for the Remington Arms Company. Its flat trajectory makes it particularly useful for varmint hunting.

ROBERTS IN LYRICS, PART V

And I feel like a bullet in the gun of Robert Ford,
I'm low as a paid assassin is.
You know I'm cold as a hired sword,
I'm so ashamed can't we patch it up,
You know I can't think straight no more.
You make me feel like a bullet, honey, in the gun of Robert Ford.

Elton John's song I Feel Like a Bullet (In The Gun of
Robert Ford), from his 1975 album Rock of Westies, makes
reference to **Robert Ford**, the notorious outlaw who shot
Jesse James.

Ford joined James's gang for a bank robbery but double-
crossed him, shooting an unarmed James in the back of the
head while he dusted a picture frame in his own home. Ford
and his brother were expecting the $10,000 reward and a
pardon for their work; in reality, they were arrested, before
being pardoned by the governor who had placed the bounty
on James's head.

ROCK 'N' ROBERTS

The Cure's **Robert Smith** (b. 1959) got into rock 'n' roll when he saw Jimi Hendrix play at the Isle of Wight festival in 1970. He took up the guitar soon after and now also plays the bass, flute, double bass, keyboard, violin and trumpet. He played bass on two Siouxsie and the Banshees records and provided the voice for a Robert Smith character in the *South Park* episode Mecha-Streisand. In the show, the gang invokes a giant Robert Smith robot to defeat a similarly huge Barbra Streisand.

Robert Hicks was an Atlanta bluesman born in 1902. He worked at a barbecue joint and sang as he served his customers, earning him the nickname **Barbecue Bob** that he used on his records.

Until the age of 19, **Robert Johnson** was just another plantation kid playing the blues at 'jook' joints to cotton-pickers in Depression-era Mississippi. Then he disappeared and re-emerged some time later with a dazzling guitar technique, becoming, in Eric Clapton's words: "the most important blues musician who ever lived."

So what happened? Legend has it Johnson met the devil at a crossroads one midnight and promised his everlasting soul in return for becoming the King of the Delta blues. Johnson only ever recorded 29 different songs, released on obscure 78rpm records. When, in 1961, they were re-released for the first time, they were a huge influence on

Clapton, **Robert Plant**, Jimi Hendrix and Keith Richards, who could not believe the songs were played by Johnson unaccompanied. Led Zeppelin later covered Johnson's Traveling Riverside Blues.

Johnson died at another crossroads in 1937 at the age of 27, probably poisoned with strychnine by a jook-joint owner jealous of Robert flirting with his girl.

West Bromwich's **Robert Plant**, more than any other person, can claim to be the spiritual father of heavy metal music – although more than a third of Led Zeppelin's songs are acoustic. The band apparently got their name when Keith Moon and Jon Entwistle of The Who suggested that a supergroup containing themselves, Jeff Beck and Jimmy Page would go down like a "lead balloon". The 'a' was taken out of 'lead' at their manager's suggestion, to stop Americans mispronouncing the name.

Not long after the release of their first album the band were forced to play a Copenhagen gig billed as 'The Nobs' when Eva von Zeppelin (an aristocratic descendant of the aeronautical inventor) objected to the album sleeve's depiction of an airship in flames. She tried to stop them using her family name in Denmark, and to cancel a TV show on which they were appearing.

Led Zep officially released no singles in the UK until 1997's A Whole Lotta Love.

Robert Fripp, the guitarist in prog-rock band King Crimson, is married to Toyah Wilcox.

Walden Robert Cassotto found fame as **Bobby Darin**, the jazz crooner who sang Mack the Knife and Beyond the Sea. Cassotto changed his name to avoid anti-Italian prejudice, supposedly choosing his new surname after seeing a broken sign at his local Chinese restaurant that read 'DARIN DUCK' rather than 'MANDARIN DUCK'. In 1968, Darin learned that his 'mother' was really his grandmother and his 'sister', fourteen years his senior, was his real mother. Darin died aged 47, while undergoing heart surgery.

Robbie Williams also covered Mack the Knife. When he covered Freedom in 1997, following his split with Take That, it reached number two in the UK charts – 26 places higher than George Michael's original. Williams has the additional honour of being the most-featured artist on the *Now That's What I Call Music!* albums. Between *Now 1* and *Now 70*, he has appeared 29 times.

Robbie started a football team, LA Vale – named after his beloved Port Vale – on his back-garden pitch in the Hollywood Hills. Player-manager Robbie took the group of Yanks and expats almost to the top of the Los Angeles Super Metro League.

Todd Haynes' 2007 film *I'm Not There*, employed six
people to play the enigmatic **Bob Dylan**, including
Heath Ledger, Cate Blanchett and a 14-year-old African
American actor called Marcus Carl Franklin. Bob Dylan
is in fact played by only one man – **Robert Allen
Zimmerman**, born in 1941 in Duluth, Minnesota.
Bob reinvented himself when he dropped out of college
and hitch-hiked to New York, and he hasn't stopped
reinventing himself since.

According to the internet-based Dylan Covers Database,
there are more than 23,000 known recorded covers of
Dylan songs and counting; more than 750 of these are
Blowin' in the Wind.

Dylan, who was secretly married to his backing singer
Carolyn Dennis for six years, was awarded an honorary
degree by St Andrews University in 2004.

The Charlatans' original keyboard player, Hammond
wizard **Rob Collins**, was jailed for four months for driving
the getaway car in an off-licence robbery. He claimed he
didn't know that his passenger had crime in mind until
he heard a gunshot inside the shop, and admitted that he
shouldn't have let his mate get back in the car afterwards.
Rob later tragically died, aged 31, in a car accident
returning to a Welsh studio from a local boozer while
recording Tellin' Stories in 1996. Just one week later, the
band supported Oasis at Knebworth.

Apart from being a one-man crusade against global poverty, former Boomtown Rat **Robert Frederick Zenon Geldof** has also worked as a slaughter man and a pea canner. I Don't Like Mondays, which Geldof wrote, references Brenda Spencer, an American teenager who shot eight elementary school pupils in January 1979, killing a janitor and the school's principal as they tried to shield the children. When asked why, she said: "I don't like Mondays. This livens up the day."

A rock 'n' roll lifer, **Bobby Gillespie** was a roadie for Altered Images, played the bass in The Wake and the drums (standing up) in The Jesus and Mary Chain before singing in Primal Scream. The band's third album, Screamadelica, won the inaugural Mercury Music Prize in 1991.

Bobby was accused in 2006 of supporting Hamas when he defaced a 'Make Poverty History' poster so that it read 'Make Israel History'. "No," he replied, "I support Celtic."

———◆———

SOULFUL ROBERTS

Robert Knight is a soul singer best known for his version of Everlasting Love. In 1968 a cover version by Love Affair topped the UK charts, in doing so denying Knight a number-one spot for a follow-up single.

R Kelly, known to his mother as **Robert Sylvester Kelly**, struck gold with hits including I Believe I Can Fly and Ignition. However, Kelly has also released Trapped in the Closet, a 22-part ongoing 'hip-hopera' starring the actor singing his way through a story of extra-marital affairs. Chapter Four ends with the cliff-hanger line: 'Pull back the cover, oh my God, a rubber!' Chapter Nine, meanwhile, stars a woman called Bridget being unfaithful with a midget.

Blue-eyed soul boy **Robert Palmer** recorded his first album in New Orleans backed by The Meters, in 1974, before turning to the smooth 1980s sounds he's best known for. His most famous song, Addicted To Love, has been a staple of Tina Turner's live performances since its release; it was originally intended as a duet with Chaka Khan but her vocal was never used due to record-label complications.

Kicked out of the boy band New Edition for his lewd antics on-stage, **Robert Barisford Brown** – known to his fans as **Bobby Brown**, 'the King of New Jack Swing' – nevertheless had a long solo career, topped by the smash hits My Prerogative (1988), Every Little Step (1989) and On Our Own (1989), the theme tune to *Ghostbusters 2*.

Brown's relationship with Whitney Houston, his wife for 15 years, was punctuated by drug abuse and brushes with the law. In the space of one year, Bobby was twice arrested while watching his daughter perform in high school cheerleading competitions – the first time in March 2006, for minor motor vehicle offences, the second in February 2007, for failing to show up at a child support hearing.

--->◆<---

CLASSICAL ROBERT

Robert Schumann, the 19th-century composer, had a phobia of all things metal, especially keys, and has long been supposed a schizophrenic. Late in life he had demonic visions, and ended his days in an asylum after jumping off a bridge in a suicide attempt. He was rescued from the Rhine by boatmen.

There are two more modern theories to explain his final madness: Firstly, his final mania was caused by syphilis, long dormant after an attack as a young man; secondly, that it was caused by mercury poisoning – then a common cure for syphilis.

--->◆<---

REGGAE ROBERTS

Sly Dunbar and **Robbie Shakespeare** could be the most prolific recording artists ever. It has been estimated that Sly's drums and Shakespeare's bass have been heard on more than 200,000 reggae records. They have appeared on rhythms for virtually every prominent Jamaican artist, from Sean Paul and Beenie Man to Peter Tosh and Gregory Isaacs, as well as Ben Harper, **Bob Dylan**, Grace Jones and Sting.

Nesta Robert Marley was born in Nine Mile, St Ann, Jamaica in 1945, and he was known as such until a Jamaican passport officer swapped his first and middle names round. **Bob Marley** moved to Kingston in his early teens and cut his first records under the name **Bobby Martell**.

After an assassination attempt while he lay sleeping in his house in Jamaica, Bob Marley moved to London and recorded Exodus. It has been suggested that Marley survived the assassination because the bullet, as it neared its target, entered a cloud of ganja smoke and forgot what it was doing.

A keen footballer, Bob died from a cancer that had spread from a wounded toe. He refused to have the toe amputated because of his Rastafarian beliefs. However, the urban myth that the injury was caused by DJ Danny Baker during a kick-around is untrue.

Bob came 12th on *Forbes* magazine's list of 2007's highest-earning dead celebrities.

ONE-HIT-WONDER ROBERTS

Bobby McFerrin had a worldwide hit in 1988 with Don't
Worry, Be Happy and then dropped off the general public's
radar – although he is actually a well-respected jazz artist.
He is an accomplished throat singer and also does a good
line in theme songs: in 1987 he sang the *Cosby Show* theme
song, and in 1993 recorded Henry Mancini's *Pink Panther*
theme music for the film *Son of the Pink Panther*.

Robert James Byrd, better known as **Bobby Day**,
had a hit with Rockin' Robin in 1958. The song reached
number two and was his only chart success. It has been
covered by The Hollies, a teenaged Michael Jackson, Lolly
and McFly.

In 1962, **Bobby 'Boris' Pickett and the Crypt-
Kickers** invited an unsuspecting world to do the Monster
Mash. **Robert Pickett** co-wrote the song, and provided
the Boris Karloff impression that helped to propel the
novelty tune to number one in the US in the two weeks
before Halloween that year. The song, which no major
label wanted to release, re-entered the US charts in both
1970 and 1973. It did not make an impact in Britain,
however, until October 1973, when it peaked at number
three.

Robert 'Bobby' Bloom had a lone hit in 1970 with
Montego Bay. The American singer-songwriter was

tragically killed in a fight over a girl, shot by a man who was never identified. His untimely death at the age of 28 left him no time to register a follow-up hit.

⊷⧫⊶

HIP-HOP ROBERTS

In the masculine, aggressive world of hip-hop, the name Robert just doesn't cut it.

Robert Matthew Van Winkle got his hip-hop moniker – Vanilla Ice – while breakdancing and rapping, moonlighting from his job washing cars.

It didn't take people long to recognise the similarities between the Ice Man's breakthrough hit, Ice Ice Baby, and Queen and David Bowie's Under Pressure. Although Van Winkle's lawyers settled with the copyright holders shortly after its release, he has only recently admitted sampling the 1981 song.

Ice, a former Florida state motocross champion, was fined $220 in 2004 when his pet goat and pet wallaroo (a cross between a wallaby and a kangaroo) escaped from his garden and it transpired that he didn't have a pet licence.

Robert Fitzgerald Diggs, better known as the RZA or Bobby Digital, is the mastermind behind the Wu Tang Clan, the group who brought East Coast hip-hop back to prominence in the early 1990s. He is obsessed with old kung fu movies and watches at least four every week. The Wu Tang Clan take its name from *Shaolin and Wu Tang* (1981), and many of RZA's songs sample kung fu dialogue.

RZA also produces film soundtracks, and is best known for Jim Jarmusch's *Ghost Dog: the Way of the Samurai* and both volumes of Quentin Tarantino's *Kill Bill.*

Robert Mwingira is a leading light in Tanzanian hip-hop, which is also known as Bongo Flava. 'Bongo' actually comes from a Swahili word, *ubongo* meaning 'brains', and does not refer to the bongo drum.

Houston's DJ Screw, aka **Robert Earl Davis Jr.**, is best known for 'screwing' songs when he remixed them. He slowed tunes, lyrics and beats to a fraction of their normal speed, creating an eerie, slurred sound that reputedly replicates the effects of the local narcotic tipple of choice, 'purple drink' or 'sizzurp', which is made by mixing cough syrup containing codeine and promethazine with fizzy soft drinks.

Users report effects ranging from slight euphoria during mild doses through to slurring, feelings of drunkenness, visual hallucinations and dissociation in larger doses. DJ Screw tragically died aged 28, in 2000, of a codeine overdose.

Other hip-hop Roberts:

Rob Swift
Rob Life
Black Rob
Rob Base
Chill Rob G

───◆───

THE ROBERTIAN DYNASTY

The **Robertian dynasty** was founded by a powerful family of Roberts in Francia, which largely corresponded to the ancient kingdom of Gaul.

Robert of Hesbaye is generally accepted to be the first Robertian. He lived in what is now Belgium around the year 800.

Robert III of Worms was Hesbaye's son. He was the Count of Worms, a city that still exists on the Rhine in Germany.

Robert IV the Strong was Worms's son. He led a revolt against King Charles in 858, fought the Bretons and died in battle in 866, defending Francia against marauding Vikings.

Robert IV's son was **Robert I of France**. Robert I's older brother, Odo, established Paris as France's capital, but had ceded the French throne to Charles the Simple in 897. Robert I was killed in single combat with Charles in 923.

Hugh Capet, the last of the Robertians, founded the Capetians, the largest and oldest royal family in Europe. The Capetians ruled France until the French Revolution in 1789, and again briefly afterwards. Other Capetians have been Latin emperors, kings of Portugal and of Spain, including Spain's incumbent King Juan Carlos. Hugh Capet's son, the second ruling Capetian, was **Robert II of France**.

⇒◆⇐

ROBERT: THE COLLEGE

Robert College of Istanbul is a highly selective boarding school in Istanbul, Turkey. It is the oldest American school on foreign soil still on its original site.

⇒◆⇐

RECORD-BREAKING ROBERTS

Robert Korzeniowski holds the Olympic record for the 20km walk, completing the course at the 2000 Sydney Games in one hour, 18 minutes and 59 seconds.

The Park Row Building is on Park Row in New York City. Designed by **Robert Henderson Robertson**, it was one of the first buildings to be called a skyscraper and was, between 1899 and 1908, the tallest office building in the world.

Standing 29 storeys high and measuring 391ft (119.2m),
it was greeted by general public acclaim, but the critical
response was lukewarm, even bad.

Architectural Review called it "detestable"; another critic
thought its blank walls "absolutely inexpressive and vacuous".
The building's engineer was called **Nathaniel Roberts**.

Robert 'Evel' Knievel is credited by the *Guinness Book of
Records* for breaking more bones during his lifetime than any
other person: 433.

Robbie Williams holds the record for the most concert
tickets sold in one day – 1.6 million for his 2006 world tour,
on November 19th 2005. He also holds the record for most
Brit Awards won and the highest number of UK chart
number-one albums by a male solo artist.

American **Robert Curbeam** holds the record for the most
spacewalks – four – during a single voyage.

Standing at 8ft 11.1ins (2.72m) tall, **Robert Wadlow** is the
tallest person whose height has been indisputably verified.
Wadlow had an enlarged pituitary gland, which caused his
growth to accelerate at a very early age – at 18 months he
weighed 62lbs, and a nine-year-old Wadlow, already over six feet
tall, is reported to have carried his father up a flight of stairs.

Robert never stopped growing, and his height was regularly measured. Just 18 days before his death the final measurement was taken. His shoe size was a 37(US) and each of his hands, from the wrist to the tip of his middle finger, was over a foot long. In 1940 a blister he got on his foot while on a professional engagement for his shoe sponsors became infected. It never got better and he died at the age of 22. Wadlow was buried in a half-ton coffin that was surrounded by solid concrete to discourage ghoulish souvenir seekers from disturbing the body.

<hr />

SILVER SCREEN ROBERTS

Back to the Future (1985) was inspired by writer **Bob Gale** finding his father's year-book and wondering what it would be like to be friends with his young dad. He wrote the film with **Robert Zemeckis**, who also directed, and the duo claim the film's last lines were a throwaway ending: they didn't intend to make any sequels and were surprised by the film's success.

Robert Mitchum had a good singing voice and sang his parts in films such as *The Night of the Hunter* (1955) and *River of No Return* (1954) instead of miming and relying on hired singers. He released an album of calypso music called Calypso – Is Like So… in 1957 and a country album, That Man, Robert Mitchum Sings, a decade later.

Robert Patrick, best known as the shape-shifting T-1000 in *Terminator 2*, also appeared in the music video for Objects in the Rear-view Mirror may Appear Closer than They Are by Meat Loaf.

Gary Graver is best known for being Orson Welles' final cinematographer. He shot the genius' unreleased *The Other Side of the Wind* and also *F for Fake*. While not working with Welles he directed adult films under the pseudonym **Robert McCallum**.

Italian director **Roberto Rossellini** was named the "father of neo-realism" by influential journal *Cahiers du Cinéma*, after his 1945 film *Roma, città aperta (Rome, Open City)* heralded a new direction for post-war cinema. Rossellini's film education started early: his father owned the Corso, Rome's first cinema, and Roberto had a free pass as a child.

Robert Moore, besides being a Tony-award-winning Broadway director, also directed the 1976 detective spoof *Murder by Death*. This send-up of country mysteries *à la* Agatha Christie featured a rare acting performance by Truman Capote, writer of *In Cold Blood* and *Breakfast at Tiffany's*.

"Here's looking at you, kid." **Robert Sacchi**, born 1941, makes a good living out of playing Humphrey Bogart, whom he closely resembles.

Robert Thorn was the US ambassador, as played by
Gregory Peck in *The Omen* (1976). Unlike Robert, the Devil's
son of medieval legend whom we met earlier, Thorn is father
to the Devil's son, Damien. Or, more precisely, not his father.

In the 2006 remake, Robert Thorn was played by Liev
Schrieber.

Robert Wagner and **Rob Lowe** played Number Two,
in the 1960s and 1990s respectively, in Mike Myers' *Austin
Powers: The Spy Who Shagged Me* (1997). Lowe grew up just
a few doors down from the Sheens. Emilio Estevez, Martin
Sheen's son, was a fellow member of the infamous 'Brat
Pack', and Lowe later starred in the *West Wing* with Martin.
In between *St Elmo's Fire* (1985) and career resurrection with
Myers, he hit a nadir when a sex tape appeared of him
having a threesome with an underage girl – although he
hadn't known she was a minor.

OSCAR-WINNING ROBERTS

Best Picture

1976   Sly Stallone's *Rocky*, produced by **Robert Chartoff** and Irwin Winkler, carries away the Best Picture Oscar. When the producers tried to buy the script from Stallone for a staggering $350,000, the penniless unknown actor refused to sell unless he was contracted to star in the film.

1974   **Robert Evans**, one of Hollywood's slickest producers, accepts the Oscar for *Chinatown*. Made from a script by **Robert Towne**, the film's dark ending is Polanski's own – he was still reeling from his wife Sharon Tate's murder by followers of Charles Manson. In the midst of 1974's success, Evans somehow managed to turn down *Jaws* when the project was offered to him.

Best Director

1994   **Robert Zemeckis** wins with *Forrest Gump*.

1980   Schmaltz-fest *Ordinary People* somehow outdoes Martin Scorsese's *Raging Bull* to give director **Robert Redford** his only Oscar. Redford was turned down for the Ben Braddock role eventually occupied by Dustin Hoffman in *The Graduate* (1967) because director Mike Nichols didn't think it was convincing that Redford would have trouble getting the girl.

1979   **Robert Benton**'s *Kramer vs. Kramer* beats *Apocalypse Now* and **Bob Fosse**'s *All That Jazz*.

1972   **Bob Fosse** wins with *Cabaret*. Fosse also won nine Tony awards, the Oscars of the theatre world: eight for choreography and one for direction.

1965   **Robert Wise** wins for *The Sound of Music* and, four years earlier, for *West Side Story*, which he co-directed with Jerome Robbins.

Best Actor

1992   **Roberto Benigni** wins for his performance in *La Vita è Bella (Life is Beautiful)*. The role is based on his father's experiences in Bergen-Belsen and is the first foreign-language performance to pick up the gong.

1983   **Robert Duvall** wins for playing Mac Sledge in *Tender Mercies*. His screen debut was as Boo Radley in *To Kill a Mockingbird* (1962), but he is best known for his immortal line in *Apocalypse Now*: "I love the smell of napalm in the morning."

1980   **Robert De Niro** scoops the best actor award for his performance in *Raging Bull*. De Niro's name is an anagram of 'error on bidet'. Not that you'd tell him to his face: Jake La Motta said of De Niro's boxing that he was so good he could have turned pro. De Niro has won twice out of a total of six nominations. The other came for his supporting role as a young Vito Corleone – a character that also earned Marlon Brando a best actor award.

1939   **Robert Donat** wins for *Goodbye Mr Chips*. Donat was born in Withington, Greater Manchester. He did not like filming in Hollywood and after his success in Hitchcock's *The 39 Steps* (1935), the big studios would move their productions to England to accommodate him. Donat's career was cut short by chronic asthma; the last words he ever spoke on screen were: "We shall not see each other again, I think."

Other Oscars

Robert Knudson has the most Oscar nominations and wins among Roberts. He won for his sound work on *Cabaret*, *The Exorcist* (1973) and *E.T.* (1982), and was nominated for seven more – from *A Star is Born* (1976) to *Who Framed Roger Rabbit* (1988).

Robert Blalack, who received a best visual effects Oscar for *Star Wars* (1977), also created the special effects in *Airplane!* three years later.

Whereas **Robert B. Sherman** won two Oscars for *Mary Poppins* (1964) – best original score and best song (Chim Chim Cher-ee) – the film's director **Robert Stevenson** left the 37th awards ceremony empty handed.
Perhaps the greatest Oscar also-ran Robert is **Robert**

Altman. The director of *M*A*S*H, Nashville, Short Cuts, Gosford Park* and more was repeatedly snubbed by the Academy. He was nominated seven times over his long career and never won until an honorary lifetime award in 2005. The treatment is perhaps reflected in the bitter, cynical tone of his 1992 Hollywood satire *The Player*.

Robert Downey Jr. (b. 1965) is the only actor ever nominated for portraying a previous nominee. Downey Jr. was lauded for his performance as Charlie Chaplin, but lost out on a gong in 1992 to Al Pacino in *Scent of a Woman*. Chaplin was awarded a special statuette for writing, acting, directing and producing *The Circus* at the first Academy Awards in 1928/29.

Robert: The TV Show

240-Robert chronicled the exploits of the eponymous
search-and-rescue unit of the Los Angeles County Sheriff's
Department. Despite starring improbably attractive young
deputies romping around in a 4x4 and a helicopter, the
show was cancelled in 1981 – just three episodes into its
second season – because of poor ratings.

240-Robert is the real-life call sign for the Los Angeles
County Sheriff Department's search-and-rescue and
paramedic teams.

———=>◆<=———

Small-Screen Roberts

Robert Craig-Martin's first TV role was a small one in
I, Claudius at the age of 12. He is best known for playing
swotty sneak Justin Bennett in the first series of Grange Hill,
two years later in 1978. Justin was supposed to be written
out after the first series, but he was so popular with viewers
that Robert actually stayed for five.

Robert Banks Stewart is in some way responsible for
many of the UK's most popular TV series, including:

- *The Sweeney* (scriptwriter)
- *The Avengers* (scriptwriter)
- *Doctor Who* (scriptwriter)
- *Bergerac* (writer and creator)

- *Lovejoy* (producer)
- *The Darling Buds of May* (producer)

Hailing from Melbourne, Australia, **Robert Jewell** was a Dalek operator in more than 50 *Doctor Who* episodes during the 1960s.

Though synonymous with the role, **Rob Llewellyn** wasn't the first person to play polygon-headed robot servant Kryten in *Red Dwarf*. That honour fell to David Ross, in the second series. Rob's wife, Judy Pascoe, played the android Camille in one episode of the BBC show and Rob was the only original cast member to reprise his role in the US version. Kryten's name comes from PG Wodehouse's butler character in *The Admirable Crichton*.

Robert Lindsay first made an impression as Wolfie, the Che Guevara of SW17 and the leader of the Tooting Popular Front, in *Citizen Smith*. However, as he got older the actor's roles swung politically to the right: in recent years, Robert has portrayed Tony Blair in two separate Channel 4 programmes.

SOAPY ROBERTS

Sighting of Jesus in BBC soap shocker!

Holby City's consultant nurse Mark Williams is played by
Robert Powell, who is best known for playing Jesus in
Franco Zefferelli's mini-series *Jesus of Nazareth*. He also
starred alongside **Robert Norman Davis** (Jasper Carrott)
in the spoof cop drama *The Detectives*.

Robert Robinson is the estranged son of slimy Paul
Robinson in *Neighbours*. First appearing in the UK in
2006, he is the 'evil' triplet of Elle and Cameron – often
pretending to be his trustworthy brother, to whom he
looks identical, at crucial moments. He was responsible
for bombings, kidnappings, intimidation and general bad
feeling in a torturous plotline that lasted months.

Bobby Ewing was the unforgettable JR's brother in *Dallas*.
The show was initially meant to focus on Bobby and his
wife, Pamela, but JR's ruthlessness and bad-boy persona
proved much more interesting to the scriptwriters.

CORONATION STREET

Robert Beck is married to Jane Danson, who plays long-
running character Leanne Battersby. Beck appears, himself,
every now and again, as Tony Gordon's hired thug Jimmy
Dockerson.

A small concession to the spirit of free love, **Robert Croft** was a minor *Corrie* character in 1968. He was the leader of a hippy commune that squatted in number 11 after Dennis Tanner's New Year's party. Lucille Hewitt moved into the squat, but stayed behind when the hippies left.

Stage and screen actor **Robert Dorning** played two roles in *Coronation Street*: firstly as Edward Wormold in 1965, then as Alderman Rogers in 1972.

EastEnders

Robert Kazinsky, who plays the tempestuous ladies' man Sean Slater, says that in real life he is shy with girls, admitting that he finds it difficult to chat them up and that he didn't have a girlfriend until he was 21.

Actor **Robert Cavanah** played Tommy Grant, who kissed Dirty Den's missus, Chrissie Watts, in 2004.

Emmerdale

Robert Sugden, who first appeared in *Emmerdale* in 1986 was played by **Robert Smith**. He then handed the role to Christopher Smith for 12 years. Sugden was then packed off to Spain for a few months before reappearing, this time played by heart-throb Karl Davies.

FOUNDING ROBERTS

Robert Baden Powell honed his bushcraft and scouting skills as a British army officer among the Zulu in the Natal province of South Africa. After fighting in the Boer War, he returned to Britain and wrote *Scouting for Boys*, which appeared in 1908. An international movement was born, with boys and girls spontaneously forming into Scout troops around the country. The authoritarian Powell, while not a fascist, wrote enthusiastically in his diary about *Mein Kampf*: "A wonderful book, with good ideas on education, health, propaganda, organisation etc. – and ideals which Hitler does not practise himself."

Theatre impresario **Robert Newman** hired young conductor Henry Wood in 1895 for a nightly series of 'Promenade concerts'. The first one took place on August 10th of that year and, now a part of the grand British tradition, they continue to this day.

Bobby Buckle was one of twelve grammar-school boys who attended Bible class at the same church. In 1882, they founded the Hotspur Football Club in Tottenham, north London, which went on to become Tottenham Hotspur FC.

Seven weeks before his 14th birthday Bobby was elected Tottenham's first-ever captain. He also featured on the first known team sheet, and was the club's first recorded goalscorer, in a 3-1 defeat to Grange Park on October 20th 1883.

SPORTING ROBERTS

Rugged Robert, aka **Bob Davidson**, was a Canadian ice hockey player who spent his entire career with the Toronto Maple Leafs. The Leafs are the only team in the NHL with a grammatically incorrect name.

Gravelly voiced **Bobby George** (b. 1945) found darts boring as a kid, and was a master builder specialising in laying floors until the age of 29. When younger, he used to lift a 112lb bag of cement above his head ten times, one-armed, as a party trick. Bobby built his dart-shaped house, George Hall, with his own hands and has two fishing lakes open to darts fans everywhere.

In the 2007 Canadian Grand Prix, **Robert Kubica** hit the wall at the Circuit Gilles Villeneuve in Montreal at a speed of 143mph (230kph). The Formula One driver was subjected to a maximum deceleration of 75G. Despite the horrific crash, the Pole received only light concussion, and walked out of hospital the next day.

In October 2008, **Robert Hodgson** was the only man to finish the Loch Lomond marathon. Faced with 17mph winds and abnormally cold waters, every single other competitor dropped out, one by one. Robert swam through the night to finish the 21.5-mile race in 17 hours and 48 minutes.

'The Limestone Cowboy' **Bob Anderson** had two promising sporting careers cut short by injury. Aged 20 in 1968, he was picked to represent Great Britain in the Olympic javelin event, but broke his arm before the team left for Mexico. Turning to football, Anderson played for Lincoln United, Woking Town and Farnborough Town, before a broken leg ended his career in 1970. He then went back to his first love, darts (he scored his first 180 aged five), and was world number one for several years in the late 1980s, winning the World Professional Championship once and the Winmau World Masters three years running.

<hr>

FOOTBALLERS

Robert da Silva Alameida is a Brazilian footballer who shortened his playing name – as Brazilians like to – simply to **Robert**. Apart from a short sojourn in Japan, he spent his career in his home country, winning five caps in the process.

Robbie Fowler's 120 goals in his eight years as a Liverpool player make him the fourth most prolific scorer in the history of the Premiership. Toxteth-born Fowler was a boyhood Everton fan, but signed for Liverpool when he turned professional on his 17th birthday. He holds the record for the fastest ever Premiership hat-trick – in four minutes and 32 seconds against Arsenal on August 28th, 1994.

In 2006 Fowler was the third-richest footballer in Britain, mainly thanks to a large property portfolio. This has led Liverpool fans to chant, "We all live in a Robbie Fowler house," to the tune of Yellow Submarine.

Robbie Keane is one of only a handful of players, along with **Robbie Fowler**, to have scored 100 Premiership goals.

Robert Kovač is a German-born Croatia defender. At both Bayer Leverkusen and Bayern Munich, and for his national team, he has played alongside his brother, Niko.

In 2007, former Newcastle, West Ham and England player **Rob Lee** was arrested, together with his former team-mate Warren Barton, for taking off in a Mercedes limousine. They drove off without permission during a night out after the driver stepped out on the Hackney Road, east London. Fortunately, the driver did not press charges.

Bob Chatt was credited with scoring the fastest-ever goal in FA Cup final history. Playing for Aston Villa, he put one past West Bromwich Albion's Joe Reader only 30 seconds into the 1895 final. Due to the fine weather and the large crowds, many of the spectators and press were still queuing to enter the Crystal Palace Stadium when the ball went in.

Roberto Baggio is the only Italian ever to score in three World Cups. Baggio was one of the most popular and talented players of the 1990s, winning the *Ballon d'Or* and FIFA World Player of the Year accolade in 1993. He will also be remembered for his penalty miss in the 1994 World Cup Final.

Before **Sir Bobby Robson Kt CBE** signed for Fulham in 1950, he was working as an electrician for the National Coal Board. On moving south, at his father's insistence, he found work at the Festival of Britain site while training three nights a week with Fulham.

Robson only played for three teams – Fulham, West Bromwich Albion and the Vancouver Royals – but made his name managing for the likes of Ipswich Town, England, Porto, Barcelona and Newcastle.

Bobby Barnes scored more than 100 league goals for West Ham, Swindon Town and Peterborough United, to name but a few. After his playing days he rose to become assistant chief executive of the PFA and in 2008 was named, alongside **Robbie Earle**, as one of the 30 most influential black people in English football.

Four World Cup-winning Roberts

Robert Frederick Chelsea Moore OBE became
England's youngest-ever captain in 1963, at the age of 22,
and his World Cup win was the third piece of silverware
he had lifted at Wembley, after the FA and European Cup
Winners' Cups in the two previous years with West Ham
United.

In fact, Bobby (108 caps – 90 as captain – and two goals)
could easily not have played in the World Cup Final. At the
end of the 1965/6 season, and tempted by a move to Spurs,
he was out of contract at West Ham. Only an intervention
by Sir Alf Ramsey stopped him being ineligible for the
England team. Even so, Moore's place in the final was
almost given to Norman Hunter.

Bobby Moore died on February 21st 1993, of bowel cancer,
at the age of 51. Just seven days earlier he'd commentated
alongside Jonathan Pearce on England's 6-0 drubbing of
San Marino at Wembley.

Younger brother to Jack, **Bobby Charlton** became a
fixture in the Manchester United team in 1957 while doing
his national service in Shrewsbury. The following year
Charlton was one of the 23 survivors of the Munich air
disaster, which killed half of a generation of United's finest
footballers, as well as United staff and journalists travelling
home from a European Cup match against Red Star
Belgrade.

First out of hospital, Charlton helped a shell-shocked
Manchester United to the FA Cup Final that year, where
the depleted team lost 2-0 to Bolton Wanderers. Charlton's
record of 758 United appearances was only surpassed in
May 2008, by Ryan Giggs.

Last, but by no means least, Charlton (106 caps and 49
goals) was a member of the 1966 England team. He is also
known for pioneering the comb-over hairstyle in the 1960s.

Roberto Rivelino (92 caps and 26 goals) was called
'*El Patada Atomique*' – 'The Atomic Kick' – by fans at
the Mexico World Cup. He was known for his stinging
free kicks, the 'elastico' or 'flip-flap' move, which he
invented, and his trademark handlebar moustache.
The son of Italian immigrants scored three goals in
Brazil's successful 1970 campaign, and also played in the
1974 and 1978 tournaments. He now commentates for
Brazilian TV.

Another Brazilian left-footer, **Roberto Carlos**, has 24in
(61cm) thighs, developed by pulling farming machinery as a
child in Brazil. They are the same size as Muhammad Ali's
at his peak – the difference being that at 5ft 6ins and 10
stone, the Brazilian left-back is nine inches shorter and five
stone lighter than the boxer.

Carlos (125 caps and 11 goals) helped Brazil to a 2002
World Cup win but he will be best remembered for his
amazing swerving free kick from 35 yards against France

in *Le Tournoi* in 1997. From some camera angles, a ball boy nearer the corner flag than the goalmouth can clearly be seen ducking for cover before the ball curves back towards the goal to beat a baffled Fabien Barthez.

⇒◆⇐

GOALKEEPING ROBERTS

Robert W. Gardner was the first goalkeeper to captain an international side. Originally a forward for Queen's Park, he switched to keeper in 1872 and did not concede a domestic goal until January 1874.

Gardner helped to arrange the world's first international game, against England in 1872. He captained and picked the Scottish team, which was entirely composed of Queen's Park players, and, in some accounts of the 0-0 draw, swapped places with **Robert Smith** and finished the game up front. When Robert switched to Clydesdale in 1874, he lost the Scottish captaincy because the Queen's Park players refused to be led by someone from another team.

Gardner's opposite number (if they'd had numbers) was **Robert C. Barker**. Barker was put in goal because he was the largest and slowest of the England squad, and it was hoped his rugby experience would help his ball handling. He, too, finished the game up front, swapping with William J. Maynard on a day that England played an incredible 1-2-7 formation!

Bob Burkard had an unenviable international record. He kept goal for the USA in the 1952 Olympics. The team got trampled 8-0 by the Italians, earning instant elimination. Bob's first proper cap came in 1957, when his team lost to Canada in a World Cup qualifier. He was not asked back.

When he signed for Arsenal in 1963, **Bob Wilson** (b. 1941) became the last amateur player to play in England's top division. He became a fixture at the club, playing until 1974 and coaching Arsenal's keepers from Pat Jennings to David Seaman, until he retired after the 2002/03 season.

Bob, whose middle name is Primrose, never wore gloves during his career. He played for the England under-15 side before becoming only the second-ever Englishman to play for Scotland, by whom he was twice capped.

Robert Green, the West Ham keeper, was an academic lad who gained 10 GCSEs. He played rugby at school, where at 6ft 3ins he was the smallest of the backs in a fearsomely large team.

MORE ROBERTS WITH ODD-SHAPED BALLS

Rob Howley of Wales was one of the best scrum halves in rugby union. He won 59 caps for his country, captaining his team at the 1999 Rugby World Cup. At his testimonial match in 2005 he was joined by footballer Ally McCoist at outside half, a friend from time spent on *A Question of Sport*.

Robert Jones joins **Rob Howley** in the elite group of Welsh scrum halves who have achieved 50 or more caps. Much of his career was spent at Swansea, but he also represented Western Province (South Africa) and Bristol Rugby club sides. He played for Wales 54 times and three times for the British Lions.

England fly-half **Rob Andrew** is rightly celebrated for his kicking and defensive play, which earned him 70 caps and the captaincy (twice) for England. Less well known are his cricketing skills. Rob got a Cambridge blue and was a talented left-handed batsmen and right-arm off-break bowler. During one of the few appearance he made for Yorkshire's second XI he managed to bowl a 17-year-old Michael Atherton for a duck.

CRICKETERS

Bobby 'The Guvnor' Abel (1857-1936) was the first
England cricketer to carry his bat (open the batting and
remain not out at the end of the innings) through a Test
innings – in an Ashes match in Sydney in 1892. Abel was
only 5ft 4ins tall, and was plagued by vision problems later
in his career, eventually becoming completely blind.

Yorkshireman **Bob Appleyard** could bowl right-arm
fast-medium or spin the ball, with no apparent change in
his delivery or run-up. He was a potent force: in the 1951
season he took more than 200 county wickets. Bob lost half
a lung to tuberculosis and had to teach himself to walk
again, spending two years out of the game because of the
disease.

Robert Crawford was born in England, but has
represented Slovenia since 2002. Slovenia took to cricket
some time after 1974, when a 13 year old called Borut
Čegovnik was introduced to the sport during an extended
visit to his penpal in Birchington-on-Sea, Kent.

Robert Taylor (b. 1941), who played for Derbyshire and
England, holds the record for the highest number of first-
class dismissals: 1649 (1473 caught and 176 stumped).

In 1986, several years after retiring, Taylor was hosting a
lunch in a Lord's hospitality suite during an international

Test when word came through that wicket-keeper Bruce French had been hit on the head and hospitalised by the New Zealand attack. Taylor had gloves in the boot of his car, borrowed kit from the other players, and bravely kept wicket until replaced by **Bobby Parks**.

ROBERTO: THE RACEHORSE

Roberto (1969-1988) was an American-raised thoroughbred that won the Epsom Derby in 1972, with jockey Lester Piggott spurring him on to beat Rheingold by a head. Roberto was named after **Roberto Clemente**, a pitcher who played for Roberto's owner's baseball team, the Pittsburgh Pirates. Clemente died in a plane crash on New Year's Eve 1972 while on a mercy mission delivering aid to Nicaraguan earthquake victims.

SLAMDUNKING ROBERTS

Robert Rose, an Australian, played in the NBA for just
three minutes after signing a ten-day contract with the LA
Clippers in the 1988/89 season.

When **Bob Lanier** played basketball in the 1980s, he had
the NBA's largest feet – an American size 22.

More basketballing Roberts, by height:

Bobby Jackson	6ft 1in.
Bobby Brown	6ft 2ins.
Bobby Wilson	6ft 3ins.
Robert Garrett	6ft 3¾ins.
Bob Weisenhahn	6ft 4ins.
Robert M. Carpenter	6ft 5ins.
Bobby Simmons	6ft 6ins.
Bob Greacen	6ft 7ins.
Robert 'Tractor' Traylor	6ft 8ins.
Bobby Jones	6ft 9ins.
Robert 'Big Shot Bob' Horry	6ft 10ins.
Robert Werdann	6ft 11ins.
Robert Swift	7ft 0ins.
Robert 'The Chief' Parish	7ft 1in.

SPORTING ROBERTS AND THEIR NICKNAMES

NAME	NICKNAMES	PROFESSION
Robert Grove	Lefty	American baseball pitcher
Roberto Duràn	*Manos de Piedra* (Hands of Stone)	Boxer
Robert Meusel	Long Bob	Baseball player
Robert de Wilde	Afro Bob/The Flying Dutchman	Dutch BMX-er
Roberto Baggio	Little Buddha/ *Il Divin Codino* (The Divine Ponytail)	Footballer
Roberto Ayala	*El Ratòn* (the Rat)	Footballer
Bob Cousy	The Houdini of the Hardwood	Basketball player
Robert Weaver	Wingnut	Surfer

PUTTING ROBERTS

In 1909, **Robert Abbe Gardner** became the youngest-
ever winner of the US Amateur golf tournament at the age
of 19 years and five months. His record stood until it was
beaten in 1994 by an 18-year-old called Tiger Woods.

Gardner was an all-round sportsman, but not all of his
records lasted for so long. His pole-vaulting world record
of 13ft 1in (3.99m) stood for only a week before fellow
American Marc Wright vaulted 1¼ins (3cm) higher.
Gardner was also a national champion in a now largely
forgotten sport called rackets, which is a bit like squash.

The first year that **Bob Ferguson** won the Open – 1880 – his
prize money was £7. He is one of only four men to win the
Open three years in a row. Only one man – Peter Thomson –
has equalled his achievement since the 19th century.

"You may as well praise a man for not robbing a bank."
Thus spoke **Bob Jones** (b. 1902) upon losing a tournament
in 1925 by a single stroke – having picked up a two-shot
penalty when he disturbed his own ball in the rough.
Because nobody else saw, the marshals left the call to Bob,
who insisted that the foul must be counted.

Not only a fine sportsman, Bob was also a great player. He
was the first – and only – man to win all the four major
tournaments of his era in the same year, completing golf's
legendary Grand Slam. In 1930, when he achieved the

feat, this comprised the US and British Opens, and both countries' Amateur tournaments. Shortly after the Grand Slam he retired, aged just 28.

Roberto DeVicenzo is best remembered for a catastrophic error in the 1968 Masters. He birdied the par-four 17th hole, but his playing partner mistakenly put him down for par on the scorecard. DeVicenzo then signed the card without noticing the error and, according to PGA rules, the score stood. Without the added stroke he would have tied with the leader **Bob Goalby** to set up an 18-hole play-off the next day. Roberto took it on the chin, famously exclaiming in his broken English: "What a stupid I am!"

Two years later he received the **Bob Jones Award**, the highest accolade given by the United States Golf Association to reward distinguished sportsmanship.

Potting Robert

Robert Milkins (b. 1976) is the only Robert ever to have scored a maximum break in one of snooker's ranking tournaments. The 147 came while qualifying for the 888.com World Championship in Prestatyn in 2006. Had he completed a maximum break in the tournament proper he would have received £147,000; as it was, his prize was a mere £5,000. He lost the match 10-4 to Mark Selby, becoming only the second person ever to lose a World Championship match after making a 147 break.

Olympian Roberts

Robert Garrett was one of the early stars of the modern Olympics. The American won gold in the shot put and discus in the inaugural 1896 games in Athens, as well as silver in the long and high jumps. In preparation, Garrett hired a blacksmith to make a discus based on classical drawings, and almost gave up when the resulting lump of metal weighed more than 30lbs. His throwing style provoked laughter from spectators and the other contestants; nevertheless, his final attempt – 29.15m – was 19cm longer than his closest competitor's.

In the 1900 Olympics, he won bronze in the standing triple jump and in the shot put, despite not competing in the shot put final because it took place on a Sunday. He also entered the discus again, yet failed to place because each of his three throws hit a tree.

At Athens in 2004, **Róbert Fazekas** threw a discus over twice as far. His 71.70m effort was, however, disqualified, and the gold awarded to second-placed Lithuanian, Virgilijus Alekna, because Róbert failed to squeeze out the necessary 75ml of urine that constitutes an adequate sample for anti-doping tests.

In 1904 an American, **Robert Stangland**, bagged three bronzes: in the long, high and triple jumps.

Stockholm's Games in 1912 saw **Robert Hennet**, a Belgian, beat England's **Robert Cecil Montgomerie** to win the fencing gold.

Robert Charpentier learned his cycling skills as a butcher's boy in rural France. He helped the French team dominate at Hitler's Olympics in Berlin, 1936, winning the men's road race by cycling 100km at an average of 39kph. He also won the 4,000m team pursuit on track, and the team time trial on the road, with the help of Guy Lapebie and **Robert Dorgebray**.

At the 1968 Games in Mexico City, **Robert Beamon**, an American long jumper, took gold and inspired a new adjective – 'Beamonesque'. His jump of 8.90m (29ft 2½in) was 55cm (21¾in) further than the previous record, making him the first person to jump further than both 28 and 29 feet. The record had previously been broken 13 times since 1901 by increments of less than 15cm (6in).

The so-called 'Perfect Jump' almost took Bob out of the sandpit and the record stood for 23 years, until Mike Powell broke it in 1991. Beamon himself never jumped further than 8.22m (26ft 11¾ in) after that day.

British boxer **Robert Wells** won bronze in the 1984 summer Olympics in Los Angeles. Wells fought in the super heavyweight (91kg and above) category; his father, William Wells, boxed at the same weight in the 1968 Olympics but did not achieve a podium position.

Centre-half **Roberto Ayala** has received two Olympic medals – a silver in Atlanta 1996, where he played alongside **Roberto Sensini**, and gold in Athens, in 2004. He has captained Argentina's national football team more times than anyone else.

———◆———

UNSPORTING ROBERTS

Robert Hoyzer, a German referee, found ignominious fame in 2005 when he admitted to match-fixing in the lower reaches of the German Bundesliga.

His downfall came when he bet on a cup game between regional side Paderborn and first-division Hamburger SV – a game in which he unfairly sent off HSV striker Emile Mpenza and awarded Paderborn two dodgy penalties. Thanks to his help, Paderborn overturned a two-goal deficit and won 4-2.

Police subsequently revealed Robert's links to a Croat organised crime syndicate. Hoyzer claimed that the betting ring took in many more officials and players, even extending to the UEFA Cup. While the Croatian gamblers are thought to have made around €2m, Robert earned only €60,000 – and a 29-month jail sentence – from the scam.

For more than two years, **Dr. Robert A. Slutsky**, a radiology researcher at the San Diego School of Medicine, published one academic paper every ten days while holding down two other jobs. Even though some colleagues were happy to put their names to the pieces, suspicions eventually were aroused and Dr. Slutsky resigned. Quantity came before quality: an investigation found frauds including "numerous experiments never performed".

⟫◆⟪

ROBERTS IN LYRICS, PART VI

Dr. Robert F. Thomas,
May his name forever stand.
Dr. Thomas was a man
The Lord must have appointed,
To live among us mountain folks
In eastern Tennessee;
And he delivered more than half
The babies in those mountains.
Among those babies
He delivered me.

Dolly Parton's song **Dr. Robert F. Thomas** is on her My Tennessee Mountain Home album from 1973. Dr. Thomas was a real doctor in Sevier County, Tennessee, who travelled the back roads by Jeep, on foot and on horseback to minister to the rural poor. He did, indeed, deliver Dolly.

In 2006, Dolly pledged $500,000 towards the construction in the county of a hospital to be named after Dr. Robert.

TRIVIAL ROBERTS

Robert LeRoy Ripley was a cartoonist whose 'Believe It or Not!' newspaper cartoons related weird bits of trivia. People thrilled to hear about a Chinaman with a 14 inch horn on his forehead, or a guy named Smokey in Wisconsin who could exhale cigarette smoke through a hole in his back. His popularity was such that when, on November 3rd 1929, Ripley pointed out that America did not have a national anthem, five million people wrote to their Representatives, and The Star-Spangled Banner was officially adopted.

In 1937, Ripley published a cartoon drawn by a small boy about his beagle who liked eating glass. The boy was called Charles Schultz, and the dog was the inspiration for… Snoopy!

Bobby Badfingers is a novelty performer whose special trick is to click his fingers really fast. His small talent has taken him a long way – to appearances on *The Paul O'Grady Show* and *The Howard Stern Show* among others. Badfingers' real name is **Robert von Merta**.

Bob Burton Jr. is an American speedcuber. Speedcubers are skilled in solving Rubik's Cubes extremely fast.

BOB'S PERSONAL BESTS:

Standard Rubik's Cube	13.15 seconds
Standard Rubik's Cube, blindfolded	3 minutes, 20.75 seconds
Rubik's Magic	1.15 seconds

ROBERTS IN LYRICS, PART VII

Dolly Parton also sang about another, unidentified Robert on her Dolly Parton (Tour Edition) album. It's a classic Country and Western song of forbidden love:

Robert's appearance is something to behold,
Dressed in the finest of store-bought clothes;
My mamma sews my clothes 'cos I'm just a poor girl,
But Robert is as real as his daddy's gold.

Later in the song, Dolly bemoans her ill fate:

Robert, oh Robert if you only knew,
The same blood is flowing in both me and you;
That rich boy's your father, but he's also mine,
And my mamma's the poor girl that he left behind.

Coincidentally, Dolly's father is called **Robert Parton**.

WRITING ROBERTS

Scotland's favourite son, **Robert Burns**, wrote poems about many animals, but he was particularly fond of his pet ewe, Mailie, and wrote her an elegy when she died.

It is unlikely that Burns, who lived from 1759 until 1796, ever wore a kilt. The kilt at that time was associated with dangerous Highland clans and King George II banned kilt-wearing between 1746 and 1791, to try to promote allegiance to his rule.

Burns was also an active Freemason, a deputy master who took charge of his lodge on several occasions.

Robert Hunter is a poet, songwriter and lyricist, and was a non-performing member of the Grateful Dead. Along with Ken Kesey he was a volunteer in Stanford University's CIA-sponsored LSD experiments some time around 1962.

While **Robert A. Heinlein**, the science fiction writer, was hospitalised with tuberculosis in the 1930s, he dreamt up the idea of the waterbed. His descriptions of it in his works were so detailed that when, in the 1960s, waterbeds became popular the idea was considered un-patentable.

Robert M. Pirsig is the author of *Zen and Motorcycle Maintenance*, the philosophical account of a motorbike trip across the US that has sold millions of copies worldwide.

Pirsig says in the introduction that, "it should in no way be associated with that great body of factual information relating to orthodox Zen Buddhist practice. It's not very factual on motorcycles, either."

Robert Louis Stevenson's working title for *Treasure Island* was *The Sea Cook*. Originally meant only as an amusement for his nephew, he was advised to change the title by the editor of *Young Folks* magazine when it was bought for serialisation.

Perhaps because of persistent ill health, Stevenson used drugs including opium and cocaine. *The Strange Case of Doctor Jekyll and Mr Hyde* (published five years after *Treasure Island*, in 1886) was the product of a six-day coke binge during which the author hardly slept.

"That an invalid in my husband's condition of health should have been able to perform the manual labour alone of putting 60,000 words on paper in six days, seems almost incredible," said his astonished wife, Fanny.

Stevenson also found the time to ride a donkey through the Cévennes hills in France, but his weak chest forced him in later life to move to the tropics. He died in Western Samoa aged just 44 in 1894.

David 'Kid' Jensen, the Canadian radio DJ, is a direct descendant of Stevenson.

Robert Ludlum penned the thrillers that spawned the Bourne films starring Matt Damon. He died in 2001 but an unknown ghost-writer writes on in his name, faithfully in his style.

It is thanks to **Robert Graves** that the Greek myths and legends are so widely read in English. Aside from his popular translation, published in 1955, he wrote *I, Claudius*, and poetry inspired by his service during the First World War. He also wrote a biography of Lawrence of Arabia in which he punctured the great man's claim to have read all the books in Oxford University's library – calculating it would take 300 years to do this.

One of America's best-loved poets, **Robert Frost** was always happier down on the farm than in the literary limelight. His first published works, in fact, were treatises on poultry, which appeared in farming journals in New England between 1903 and 1905.

Robert Lochner was a German journalist who helped create a free press in West Germany after the Second World War. He also helped US President John F. Kennedy write his famous speech given in Berlin in 1963. Lochner provided phonetic spellings so the President did not mispronounce his German – including the famous phrase, *"Ish been oin bear-lee-ner"*.

Contrary to popular belief, *"Ich bin ein Berliner"* does not mean "I am a doughnut", and the urban myth is not well known inside Germany.

Robert Harris's million-selling novel, *Fatherland*, published in 1992, is a counterfactual story – it imagines what life would be like if Hitler had won the Second World War and

if traces of the Holocaust were only coming to light many years later, in a Germany ruled by the Third Reich.
Harris is married to author Nick Hornby's sister, Gill, who is also a writer.

Bob Woodward, a *Washington Post* journalist, helped to uncover the Watergate scandal in America in 1972, which eventually led to the resignation of President Richard Nixon. His anonymous FBI source, 'Deep Throat', was named after a famous porn film of the time.

Woodward was played by **Robert Redford** in *All the President's Men*, a 1976 film of the Watergate investigation.

⟫◆⟪

ROBERT: THE DICTIONARY

Le Petit Robert is the French equivalent of the *Shorter Oxford* or the *Collins Concise English Dictionary*. In 1609, **Robert Poisson** was the first man to produce a printed French dictionary.

⟫◆⟪

POETS LAUREATE

Robert Southey tends to be eclipsed by the more famous 'Lakes' poets William Wordsworth and Samuel Taylor Coleridge. He preceded Wordsworth as Poet Laureate, holding the position from 1813 until his death in 1843. Southey's most enduring contribution to literature may be The Story of the

Three Bears – the original Goldilocks story – which appeared in his 1834 novel *The Doctor.* The children's rhyme *What are Little Boys Made of?* is also attributed to him.

Robert Bridges was Poet Laureate from 1913 to 1930. He is the only medical doctor ever to have held the post: Bridges also worked in Casualty at St. Bartholomew's Hospital, London.

———◆◆◆———

LUCKY ROBERT

On the morning of November 18th 1996, two fishermen picked up a man bobbing in the chilly water two miles off the Long Island coast. **Robert Slutsky** did not remember how he got there but his family said he had left home in Far Rockaway, New York – which is not even on the coast – the night before complaining of a stomach ailment. At 300lbs in weight, Robert was well insulated, which probably saved him from dying of cold.

———◆◆◆———

UNLUCKY ROBERT

Robert Bunsen, a 19th-century chemist, almost killed himself twice with arsenic, and lost the sight in his right eye in a laboratory explosion. He did, however, achieve immortality by giving his name to the Bunsen burner.

NOBEL ROBERTS

Five Roberts who won the Nobel Prize:

NAME	YEAR	PRIZE	FOR
Robert Koch	1905	Physiology or Medicine	Work identifying tuberculosis bacilli
Robert A. Millikan	1923	Physics	Measuring the charge of an electron
Robert Robinson	1947	Chemistry	Work on plant dyes and alkaloids
Robert S. Mulliken	1966	Chemistry	Molecular orbital theory
Robert W. Fogel	1993	Nobel Memorial Prize in Economic Sciences	Cliometrics (economic history)

IG NOBEL ROBERTS

The Ig Nobel Prize, established in 1991, honours ten academics or public figures every year whose achievements "make people laugh and then make them think".

Five Ig Nobel Roberts:

1991   **Robert Klark Graham** receives the Ig Nobel Prize for Biology, for pioneering the Repository for Germinal Choice, a sperm bank that accepts donations only from Olympians or Nobel Laureates.

1993   The prize for Mathematics goes to **Robert W. Faid** of Greenville, South Carolina, for calculating the precise probability that Mikhail Gorbachev is the Antichrist. For those of you who like a flutter, the odds are: 860,609,175,188,282,100 to 1.

1994   Vet **Robert A. Lopez** inserts cat mites into his own ear and carefully observes and analyses the results, winning himself the prize for entomology.

1996   **Robert Matthews** of Aston University in the West Midlands impresses the judges with his studies into Murphy's Law (briefly: whatever can go wrong, will), and especially for demonstrating that toast often falls buttered-side down. The Ig Nobel Prize for Physics is his.

2004   **Robert Batty** of the Scottish Association for
        Marine Science shares the Ig Nobel Prize for
        Biology with distinguished colleagues from
        Sweden, Denmark and Canada. Their papers,
        one entitled 'Sounds Produced by Herring (*Clupea
        harengus*) Bubble Release', seem to prove that
        herrings communicate by farting.

LAST ROBERTS

Bob Roberts, who died in 1882, was the last captain of a British commercial vessel operating under sail. He worked the Thames sailing barges for years, eventually becoming skipper of the *Cambria*, which was sold to the Maritime Trust in 1970.

Bob came from a musical family and he became a respected folk-singer and storyteller. In 1966 he read five seafaring stories to kids on the BBC's *Jackanory*.

Nineteen-year-old **Robert Smith** was the last person to be publicly hanged in Scotland. He was executed on May 12th 1868 in Dumfries, for the murder of a young girl.

Robert Snooks was the last man to be executed in England for highway robbery, on March 11th 1802.

Robert Last was the eldest of the three Last brothers. He was a German big band drummer who played in several popular dance bands of the 1960s and 1970s. All three brothers played for the Radio Bremen dance orchestra, and in the early seventies Robert also formed his own studio orchestra, which put out a series of albums on Decca Records with titles such as Non-Stop Musical Party.

There is every chance we have missed a Robert, or two.

Let us know at **www.stripepublishing.co.uk**

Acknowledgements

I'd like to thank all the Roberts in the world, but especially **Mr. Robert Cailliau**, who co-developed the World Wide Web with Tim Berners Lee. Their vision was of a network allowing physicists at CERN to share information with other researchers.

How far we've come. Without his invention this book would not have been possible. I also owe a great debt to every single person, website, book and library that I've used as a resource.

I must also thank **Robert Taylor** and **Rupert Morris** (who will be amused to learn his name is a German variant of Robert), who have both kept me in gainful writing employment during this project.

Finally, many thanks to Dan Tester and Stripe Publishing.

Bibliography / recommended websites

Close Listening
Charles Bernstein, Oxford University Press (1998)

Dictionary of First Names
Leslie Dunkling and William Gosling, Everyman (1983)

First Names: the Definitive Guide to Popular Names in England and Wales, 1944-1994
Emma Merry, with Kay Callaghan and Chris Cotton, HMSO (1995)

The Great Betrayal: Fraud in Science
Horace Freeland Judson, Harcourt (2004)

Law and Mental Health: a Case-Based Approach
Robert G Meyer and Christopher M Weaver, Guilford Press
(2006)

The Mafia Made Easy: the Anatomy and Culture of La Cosa Nostra
Peter J De Vico, Tate Publishing and Enterprises (2007)

The Oxford Dictionary of English Christian Names
Elizabeth Gidley Withycombe, Oxford University Press
(1973)

This Thing of Darkness
Harry Thompson, Headline Review (2005)

Who Sailed on the Titanic? The Definitive Passenger Lists
Debbie Beavis, Ian Allan Publishing (2002)
www.amiright.com
www.archives.gov
www.archiveshub.ac.uk
www.bbc.co.uk
www.books.google.com
www.capitalpunishmentuk.org
www.casebook.org
www.chortle.co.uk
www.cnn.com
www.englandfootballonline.com
www.exclassics.com
www.famouspeople.co.uk
www.findarticles.com

www.forbes.com
www.guardian.co.uk
www.guinnessworldrecords.com
www.icons.org.uk
www.iht.com
www.improbable.com
www.independent.co.uk
www.imdb.com
www.listverse.com
www.nobelprize.org
www.olympic.org
www.oscar.com
www.statistics.gov.uk
www.telegraph.co.uk
www.timesonline.co.uk
www.televisionheaven.co.uk
www.urbandictionary.com
www.wikipedia.org